D0965851

# THE FREE MARKET
# CAPITALIST'S
# SURVIVAL GUIDE

# THE FREE MARKET CAPITALIST'S SURVIVAL GUIDE

## HOW TO INVEST AND THRIVE IN AN ERA OF RAMPANT SOCIALISM

JERRY BOWYER

*An Imprint of* HarperCollins*Publishers*
www.harpercollins.com

This book is designed to provide readers with a general overview of financial markets and how they work. It is not designed to be a definitive investment guide or to take the place of advice from a qualified financial planner or other professional. Given the risk involved in investing of almost any kind, there is no guarantee that the investment methods suggested in this book will be profitable. Thus, neither the publisher nor the author assume liability of any kind for any losses that may be sustained as a result of applying the methods suggested in this book, and any such liability is hereby expressly disclaimed.

THE FREE MARKET CAPITALIST'S SURVIVAL GUIDE. Copyright © 2011 by Jerry Bowyer. All rights reserved. Printed in the United States of America. No part of this book may be used or reproduced in any manner whatsoever without written permission except in the case of brief quotations embodied in critical articles and reviews. For information, address HarperCollins Publishers, 10 East 53rd Street, New York, NY 10022.

HarperCollins books may be purchased for educational, business, or sales promotional use. For information, please write: Special Markets Department, HarperCollins Publishers, 10 East 53rd Street, New York, NY 10022.

FIRST EDITION

*Designed by Renato Stanisic*

Library of Congress Cataloging-in-Publication Data
Bowyer, Jerry.
The free market capitalist's survival guide : how to invest and thrive in an era of rampant socialism / Jerry Bowyer.—1st ed.
p.   cm.
ISBN 978-0-06-182483-8
1. Capitalism—United States. 2. Free enterprise—United States. 3. Economics—Political aspects—United States. 4. Investments—United States. I. Title.
HB501.B7379   2011
332.60973—dc22          2010018762

11   12   13   14   15      OV/RRD      10   9   8   7   6   5   4   3   2   1

# Contents

*Introduction: Still in the Woods*  xi

CHAPTER 1 Not Clinton  1

No Centrism  2
Bail 'Em and Nail 'Em  12
No Newt  15

CHAPTER 2 Obamanomics 101  19

CHAPTER 3 Applied Obamanomics  25

The Japanese Ghost Economy  25
Gradual Nationalization  28
How Bad Could Things Get?  35

CHAPTER 4 **You Are Here** 43

That '70s Show 43
Not Giving Credit Where Credit Is Due 47
Dis-Integration 50

CHAPTER 5 **Principles for Surfing the Socialism** 61

Move Taxes to Center Stage 62
Time to Get Small 75
Investing in a Jobless Recovery 79
The Catacomb Economy 81
M&A Is the New IPO 89
Angels and Profits 97
Act Globally 109
Acres of Diamonds Strategy 115

CHAPTER 6 **Debt Investment Strategies** 123

Bonds Prefer Gentlemen 123
The Municipal Bond Complex 128
Inflated Expectations 138

CHAPTER 7 **Equity Investment Strategies** 143

How to Surf the Green Recession 143
Media Suppression Workarounds 153
The Political Bull Market 166
Planes, Trains, Automobiles, and Other Suckers' Bets 177
Get Real (Estate) 181

CHAPTER 8 The Bush Boom, Bust, and a
New Birth of Freedom  193

Our Great Civic Revival  202

*Acknowledgments*  207
*Index*  209

# Introduction: Still in the Woods

You are not out of the woods yet. I know about the Republican electoral momentum . . . and about the legislative resistance to some of the president's agenda . . . and about the adaptability of American entrepreneurs. Like you, I've read the sanguine analysis of Obamacare and the alleged overreactions of its opponents. I know all about the Tea Partiers, too; in fact, I am one of them myself. None of those facts will prevent the era of economic malaise and financial disruption through which you and I must pass.

Anyone who thinks we dodged a bullet on health care has failed to gather the proper intel about the weapons we face. Obamacare is not something that flows from the barrel of a conventional firearm; it is much more like an agent of biological warfare. It does not explode out of the barrel and either immediately hit (or miss) you. Its effects spread—gradually. It emerges from the original enabling legislation and spreads down through the heavily left-of-center bureaucracy at HHS and the IRS and all the other acronyms that end with an *s* but don't actually produce any palpable services.

The simple truth is that no matter what else passes the legislature and no matter how many congressional seats change hands, America elected a president who was outside of the mainstream of our political culture, and the office of president is a very powerful one in our constitutional system. It was designed that way as a reaction to the extremely weak executive powers inherent to the Articles of Confederation. The powers inherent to our chief executive are found largely in Article II of the Constitution and they are considerable. So the loss of firm control of the legislative branch by the party in charge of the White House may be a setback for the Obama agenda, but only a partial one. Presidents who are hostile to the American tradition of free enterprise can do quite a bit of damage on their own with the powers that are explicitly granted to them.

But our troubles are even worse than that, because we have a president who does not consider himself to be limited only to the powers that have been granted to him. He is not limiting himself to the powers enunciated in Article II. He understands that the founders of our country held a conception of government consistent with "negative liberties"—that is, freedom from government intrusions—instead of one consistent with "positive liberties"—that is, entitlements to government services. But going back at least as far as his days on the faculty of the University of Chicago Law School, he has rejected the founders' view in favor of a more expansive and redistributionary role for the national government.

Such a president can wreak havoc upon health care, energy, labor, insurance, financial, and telecommunications markets. He can use the enormous purchasing power of the federal government to punish non-union, non-green, non-domestic, non-"patriotic," and otherwise noncompliant businesses. He can use the enormous powers of the office of Attorney General to enforce vague statutory prohibitions against anticompetitive, predatory, and manipulative market actors. Such a president can do this, and much more, without the approval of Congress.

As of this writing, the president and his team have already begun to launch such "legislative bypass operations"—that is, policy initiatives that bypass the traditional Article I role of the legislature and govern economic life progressively more and more through executive orders, initiatives, and regulatory rule-making powers.

Only the courts stand as a possible bulwark against such executive powers' incursions into the private economy, and, unfortunately, the courts have mostly surrendered in those battles since the late 1930s. No prudent investor would dream of depending on either the self-restraint of the administration nor the external restraint of the judiciary as a protection against such market disruptions.

Nor would any prudent investor ignore the threats coming from another branch of government, which is neither entirely executive nor entirely legislative, neither entirely public nor entirely private. The Federal Reserve System, especially the Federal Open Market Committee (FOMC), which determines our money supply through open market operations, represents nearly as large a risk factor as do executive actions. The Fed controls the monetary base, the money out of which the members' banks derive the money that we all save and spend. By extension, it controls the level of inflation, speculation, and the value of the dollar relative to other currencies. As of this writing, Fed policy is the most expansive of our lifetime, perhaps of our peacetime history. More congressional Republicans won't save us from that; in fact, it is Republicans who gave us

Dr. Bernanke and his magical money machine. Much of that monetary base has already moved out of reserves and into our economy. Much more of it probably will. You are already in a high-risk environment for inflation.

These are not easy predictions for me to make—I'm an optimist. For years I've been the guy whom TV and radio producers call when they're looking for someone to counterbalance a doomsayer they've booked for their programs. I've debated the "coming collapse"-ers and the "looming depression"-ers, the gold bugs, and the Y2K profiteers. I've done this during Republican and Democratic administrations. They were wrong under Reagan; they were wrong under H. W. Bush; they were wrong under Clinton; and they were wrong under seven years of W. Bush. There were, of course, recessions amid those decades of boom, but nothing like the Armageddons and apocalypses on which newsletter publishers, numismatists, and assorted authors have made a handsome living.

Things are different now. I'm still an optimist. I believe that with God's grace, a little wisdom, and a lot of courage, America will come to her senses. In the meantime, your world has changed before your eyes. Let me make it more personal: This is not just a matter of reading unusual words in the newspaper like "nationalize" or "judicial modification" or "expropriation"; your daily life is changing right now. So is mine.

I've been thinking about this event for a long time. At a key time in my childhood I was raised by my paternal grandparents, who had lived and suffered through the Great Depression. They communicated to me through stories, and through their own frugal ways, the sense of scarcity that they brought with them out of that time of national crisis. My grandfather was a socialist and a small business owner at the same time. I guess both came from the same root: a mistrust of corporate

America. When he died, I read his books and became a Fabian socialist like Pop-Pop.

I threw myself into the study of economics and politics. I read the economics classics of the Right and the Left starting in my early teens. Eventually, I moved on from theoretical economics to accounting and then finance. I wanted to understand how wealth is created and destroyed. I wanted to understand why the Great Depression occurred and how to avoid another. I researched to find out whose predictions had been right about that terrible tragic contraction in the 1930s, and who had failed to see it coming. I asked similar questions about the stagflationary '70s and the booming '80s and late '90s. Who saw it coming? Who got it right? Who got it wrong?

It took almost a decade to figure out that Pop-Pop was wrong about socialism. It took two more decades to learn that he was right about entrepreneurialism. This book is about both. It is about how to use the latter to survive and overcome the former.

You will not find lists of investments in this book. I've read scores of books about finance and investing, and very few of them have lists of stocks and bonds to buy. That's how it should be. A good investment can turn into a bad investment in less than a minute; all it has to do is see its price appreciate from a level of undervaluation to a level of overvaluation. Stock tips are for newsletters, or now perhaps only for e-mails and Twitter. Good investment books are not built on tips; they're based on principles. You will be the judge of whether this book is a good investment book, but I assure you that it is a book based on principles. I have, to the best of my ability, reasoned through to these principles. I may well be wrong about many things, but like an obedient algebra student, I've shown all my steps. If I'm wrong, you'll find it easier to see where the error crept in.

. . . .

HERE, IN SUMMARY form, are some of the principles you will
need to follow to prosper under the current anti-wealth climate:

1. Leftism won't work; don't invest in it. The general drift
   of "enlightened" opinion has been in Obama's favor.
   His efforts to revive the economy have been treated as
   plausible, if not definitive, successes. Don't believe it. A
   centrally planned economy will lag well behind a free
   one. Investment bets on the success of the program are
   unwise. The general practice of investing in all things
   American should be put on hold until this fleeting
   moment of lunacy passes.

2. Don't invest in the specific industries that the politicians are focused on. When Washington decides to fix
   or "reform" an industry, sell your interest in that industry. Don't try to take advantage of bailouts or subsidies.
   Those things are rewards for friends of the regime. For
   you, on the other hand, they are bait. Don't take it.

3. Invest in solutions to leftism. Central planning creates
   many problems, unintended and otherwise. Invest in
   solutions to those problems. Help taxpayers, carbon-
   based energy consumers, politically disfavored media
   outlets, and people who depend on private health care.

4. Invest in alternatives to the institutions destroyed by the
   Left. Look at investments in alternatives to any institution that is the subject of "reform." If government
   decides to fix the big banks, sell them and buy small

banks, or bank alternatives. As government gradually nationalizes large health care conglomerates, move toward alternatives.

5. When the government hates things that are big, be small. Don't invest in anything big enough that the state sees it as a rival to its own power.

6. When the government trashes contracts, invest in people who don't need them. The extended chains of legally binding agreements that link the world of investment are being dissolved by legal doctrines that question the sanctity of contracts. This places a premium on trust relationships over legal ones.

7. Find cities of refuge. There are kinds of investments that the Left will not attack. Perhaps these investments are politically sacrosanct. Perhaps, as in municipal bonds, private involvement is a necessary part of their grander design. Or maybe, in the case of foreign markets, they lie outside the reach of our leaders. Try, wherever practical, to place your wealth in those zones that are insulated from the tax man and the regulator.

8. An inflationary dollar changes every single transaction in which you engage. Money loses value every moment that you hold it. Protect yourself by shifting assets away from those that pay you a future promised quantity of dollars—such as domestic stocks and bonds. Shift your wealth toward assets that pay you a quantity of something else, ounces of a commodity, or units of a different currency.

9. When dealing with dollar-yielding assets be aware of the distortions created when something that is supposed to be a stable unit of measure becomes an unstable one. A central bank that manipulates the value of money is analogous to a Bureau of Weights and Measures that fluctuates the length of a foot or the weight of an ounce. The financial statements of any U.S. company in which you invest will all be distorted by this effect. If you don't understand the nature of those distortions, don't invest in the company.

ONE THING SEEMS certain to me: There is pain ahead. Socialism is a violation of the iron laws of human nature. It is a source of misery. The people have voted for security over liberty and for living off the sweat of another man's brow. I don't believe that if my grandfather had lived through the 1970s that he would have remained a socialist. He was always learning, and I think he would have learned, as did millions of small business owners, from the pain. America will have to learn, as have so many hundreds of millions around the world, about the false promises of socialism, the "god" that failed.

I pray that this book would spare you and yours some of that pain.

# THE FREE MARKET
# CAPITALIST'S
# SURVIVAL GUIDE

# CHAPTER ONE

# Not Clinton

B arack Obama is a Fabian socialist who prefers a centrally planned economy to one in which the decisions are made by investors, entrepreneurs, and consumers. Fabian socialists differ from their revolutionary comrades in that they are committed to gradualism as a strategy. That was the case a hundred years ago when Fabianism first emerged, and it is even more the case now that socialism has been discredited in the eyes of the masses around the world. Fabians know that socialism scares people, and so they use their propaganda tools to project an image of moderation.

Initially Obama had appointed a number of moderates to positions of high visibility in his economic team. But when pressed by media to reveal whether he will back off of his tax hike pledges, he refuses to endorse anything more than a delay in hiking taxes. He will hike taxes, he said; it's not a matter of whether, but of when. Members of the financial press, who tend to understand economics (at least a little) better than the generic press corps, seem unwilling to accept this answer. How could he stick to a tax hike pledge in the middle of cataclysmic financial disruptions? Some of them are personal acquaintances and even friends, and I have seen them gradually move from denial to acceptance. Obama is not a moderate, and now everyone knows that.

Why did it take so long for so many to come to that conclusion? It is because they failed to follow the Obama line of reasoning. Obama genuinely believes that markets have collapsed because they have been given too few regulatory restrictions. He genuinely believes that business has contracted because of the Bush tax cuts of 2003. If that is the case, why wouldn't he have stuck to his regulatory and taxing agenda?

## No Centrism

Yes, he has spoken favorably about some of the things that Clinton did, but not about Clinton's centrist initiatives. Obama apologists have tried to appropriate the economic outcomes of the Clinton administration, but only because they wrongly believe that Clinton's modest tax hikes on the wealthy in 1993 caused the boom that occurred later that decade. However, deep down there are some important differences between Clinton and Obama. Clinton had already recast himself as a Southern moderate long before he ran for president. Clinton had not come up through Hyde Park leftism, like Obama, into a brief stint as senator and Democratic presidential primary aspirant. Clinton came up through a culturally conservative Southern state. He gained and then lost the office of Attorney General, an inherently conservative law-and-order post. He had his crisis early, and that crisis forced him to conform to the politics of his state.

Obama has not suffered any comparable political crises so

far, and certainly none that required a shift to the center. He came to the most powerful political, economic, and military post in human history with his leftism quite intact. It will not be surrendered without a life-transforming leadership crisis and a struggle.

Some of my colleagues were wrong to predict a shift to the center. They forgot one of the fundamental principles of modern presidential policy forecasting: Don't be fooled by moderate appointments, especially cabinet ones. A new presidency is like a new kitchen—the cabinets are for show. The real story is behind the cabinets. In the modern presidency, staff positions trump constitutional offices. Look to the chief of staff most of all—a hyperpartisan attack dog named Rahm Emanuel. Some hopeful investors took solace in the appointment of a moderate like Tim Geithner as treasury secretary. They argued that he would be a moderating influence on President Obama, but the treasury secretary has shown himself to be a company man, standing on the podium and smiling and nodding his way through presidential remarks that come roaring out of the environs of the Far Left.

Besides, Geithner is busy running the financial world. Former secretary Henry Paulson (a captive of his own leadership path, as we all are if left to ourselves) left Goldman Sachs to come to the Treasury Department, which he quickly turned into a giant Goldman Sachs. The only thing Paulson has ever done in his career was to build and maintain a giant investment bank, so in a time of crisis, he went back to his baseline and re-created his old job at his new job. Secretary Geithner is, among other things, the CEO of the world's largest investment bank, formerly known as the Treasury Department. He will have his head and hands full running this new financial behemoth, and he is dealing with the ripples of ripples of ripples that come with any government intervention into the market. Geithner is unavailable for the task of creating America's new economic program.

For that, Obama will stay at home. No need to go next door to Treasury when he'll have his economic team right downstairs. Lawrence Summers may have been a moderating influence on the tendency to overregulate and overtax, but in the end those decisions have been political ones. Geithner and Summers and Christina Romer and the rest of the gelded moderates have so far been brought in at the end, to stand near (but not too near) the podium for the announcement of yet another Five-Year Plan. The Left has been running the Congress and they have wanted to please their constituents back home. Members of the House of Representatives don't have a four-year cushion before facing the voters again. They've got two years, which in today's world means they have no cushion at all. The Left is going to want something, and they seem to have an inordinate interest in hurting wealthy people. They simply won't stand for a renewal of the Bush tax cuts. They won't stand for CEO pay to be left alone.

The Obama playbook has involved enormous increases in public spending. Summers won't resist that; he was one of the first public voices to call for the stimulus that was enacted in 2008. Summers believes, as does Obama, that spending—not production—is the chief measure of economic health. As of the time of this writing, there seems to be no effectively functional voice of spending restraint in the West Wing. Yes, Peter Orszag of the Office of Management and Budget (OMB) has some history of squawking about deficits. I've debated him myself on this issue, but in the final analysis the deficit hawks in the Democratic Party are really arguing more for tax hikes than for spending cuts. And Orszag recently quit anyway.

Forget Obama's calm demeanor. A good friend of mine wrote an open letter to the president-elect during the transition period in which he expressed the belief that maybe Obama was more moderate than my friend had feared. Why did he change his mind? Obama's calm demeanor. I told my friend to stop looking at the faces of politicians, who tend to be less scrutable than World Series of Poker champions. FDR emitted an air of confidence and recovery as he enacted policies that took a short recession and turned it into the longest depression in U.S. history. Yes, we want our president to be calm; but more than calmness, we want wisdom. If personality could trump law, taxes, and regulation, then the Great Depression would have ended in 1932 instead of 1942.

Yes, Reagan was a sunny optimist, but he was an economically literate sunny optimist. He didn't grin us into the booming '80s, he governed us into them. The grin just told us that he enjoyed it.

If, against my expectations, Obama ever shifts to the center, the structure of his arguments will change. Obama is a reasonable man. I don't mean that he holds reasonable views. I mean that he thinks in syllogisms and expresses them out loud in paragraphs; he really does explain himself. The trick (which really is no trick at all) is to listen carefully to what he actually says. Don't look for code words, or signals, or "dog whistles," or any of the other chicken entrails that pundits use to ply their professions. Listen to the "we should do A, because of B, C, and D." His policy will shift when his thinking shifts, and since he likes to talk to the press, he will do it in full view.

Obama is not afraid to speak his mind. Many politicians are, and for good reason. They've been burned by a press corps that takes their quotes out of context (or even worse, in context) to create "gotcha" headlines. That's why so many politicians babble those inane talking points that we hate so much. They call it "message discipline." Bush, for instance, knew that if he started winging it, he would get into trouble. Knowing his limitations, he stopped winging it. Obama doesn't know his limitations. He's not afraid to think out loud. And he likes the sound of his own voice. He likes the sound of his own thoughts in his own voice. It's not that he lets his guard down when he speaks; it's that he doesn't really have guards to begin with. It's refreshing that he speaks his mind. More than that, it is useful for investors like us to be able to peer into his mind and spot the shifts and turns, which we can leverage to preserve and expand our capital.

So, WHAT WOULD a shift sound like?

First, let's learn to read the president's rhetoric without illusions.

During the second presidential debate, candidate Obama was asked questions by ordinary citizens in a town-hall format. The first came from a man named Allen Shaffer:

ALLEN SHAFFER: With the economy on the downturn and retired and older citizens and workers losing their incomes, what's the fastest, most positive solution to bail these people out of the economic ruin? . . .

OBAMA: It means that we are cracking down on CEOs and making sure that they're not getting bonuses or golden parachutes as a consequence of this package. And, in fact, we just found out that AIG, a company that got a bailout, just a week after they got help went on a $400,000 junket.

And I'll tell you what, the Treasury should demand that money back and those executives should be fired. But that's only step one. The middle class needs a rescue package. And that means tax cuts for the middle class.

It means help for home owners so that they can stay in their homes.

In order to recognize the redistribution philosophy in Obama's answer, one must learn to understand the algebra of his rhetorical style—that is, you must learn to practice substitution for his verbal variables. The best example is "middle-class tax cut." A large proportion of the people who get a check from the federal government pay little or no federal income taxes. Therefore, the check they get from Uncle Sam cannot possibly be honestly treated as a refund; therefore the amount of the check that exceeds the taxes paid is a transfer payment, not a refund. A tax proposal that takes more money from high earners and gives that money, in the form of a transfer payment, to moderate earners is no different in substance from traditional left-leaning redistributionist policies of the past. The only difference is rhetorical.

Substitute "transfer payment" for "tax cut" and you find candidate Obama proposing a general transfer payment to the middle class in order to stimulate the economy, and some sort of targeted transfer payment to delinquent home owners to stave off foreclosure. Note, especially, the "pivot." The candidate was not asked a question about the middle class or even about economic recovery. He was asked about the financial rescue package. His mind went automatically to transfer payments as a cure to the financial disruptions on Wall Street.

Obama was clearly an advocate of trickle-up economics

prior to the election, but did that change once he was elected? Many people think so; I do not. First of all, such a transition is, on the face of things, generally implausible. Liberal candidates move left during the primaries, right during general elections, and back left when in office. If a tilt right comes at all, it comes in the run-up to reelection, or (like Clinton) after a punishing midterm election. The wise investor kept a very close eye on the 2010 congressional races for a hint into Obama's future policy direction. That election changed nothing.

President-elect Obama's rhetoric did not shift after his own election. His first press conference focused on economic matters. As he stood at the podium, a collection of (generally moderate) financial statesmen stood behind him. Like props in a stage play, none of them had been given a speaking part.

All of the lines were spoken from the holder of the "office of the president-elect." He reaffirmed his commitment to the redistributionist model, explicitly rejecting the possibility that he would reverse his position on taxes: 95 percent would get their checks, 5 percent would pay for those checks. Consumers would be stimulated. His campaign position was right, and was all the more necessary in a time of crisis. A meeting with some of the great economic minds of the Democratic Party had no discernible effect on President-elect Obama.

Nor, apparently, did his choice of key advisors alter his redistribution plans. As media apologists were waxing eloquent about the centrist credentials of former Clinton treasury secretary Larry Summers, Obama was explaining precisely why he had invited Summers to join him in the West Wing:

> We'll need to bring together the best minds in America to guide us. And that is what I've sought to do in assembling my economic team. I've sought leaders

who could offer both sound judgment and fresh thinking, both a depth of experience and a wealth of bold new
ideas—and most of all, who share my fundamental belief
that we cannot have a thriving Wall Street without a
thriving Main Street; that in this country, we rise and
fall as one nation, as one people. . . .

Larry Summers also brings a singular combination
of skill, intellect, and experience to the role he will play
in our administration. . . . He also championed a range
of measures, from tax credits to enhanced lending programs to consumer financial protections that greatly
benefited middle-income families.

As a thought leader, Larry has urged us to confront
the problems of income inequality and the middle-class
squeeze, consistently arguing that the key to a strong
economy is a strong, vibrant, growing middle class.

This idea is at the core of my own economic philosophy and will be the foundation of all of my economic
policies.

Forgive the long quote, but it is important, if you are to
be able to discern a shift in investment climate, that you learn
not just to identify Obama's positions on issues but to read the
structure and flow of his thought as well. When Obama speaks
in terms of national unity, he is brilliantly recasting class warfare as unity.

Genuine classical free-market economics does recognize that we stand or fall together; that Wall Street needs
Main Street, and that Main Street needs Wall Street. But
that is not the point that the president has continually made.
Notice in the quote above that our national unity is unidirec-
tional: Wall Street needs Main Street, period. If Wall Street

is hurting, it's not because U.S. corporate tax rates are higher than in the rest of the developed world, or that a wave of financial regulation post-Enron has driven financial activity to London and Dubai. No, it's because there have not been enough transfer payments to the "middle class." What does Wall Street do for Main Street? As far as Obama's rhetoric is concerned—nothing. We're left to believe that financial markets are non-contributing—even parasitical—elements of our economy.

Summers's job, then, was not to deregulate the banking sector—as he did under Clinton—but to oversee the redistribution of wealth to consumers. His job was not to oversee a cut in the tax rate on capital gains—as he did in 1997—but to oversee an increase, the proceeds of which (if there are any) have been transferred to politically favored classes and businesses. If there are no proceeds from the higher capital gains taxes, at least a sense of "fairness" is created. The populist mob will have been mollified.

The announcement of Summers was conspicuously empty of any of the pro-growth elements of the program he helped implement under President Clinton. Tax cuts, trade liberalization, deregulation, and welfare reform were MIA. We were expected to believe that the boom of the late '90s came about because Summers spoke, from time to time, about income inequality.

Some investors bought into the symbolism of the choice of Summers as an economic advisor, but that turned out to be a suckers' bet. The rally quickly abated as it became clear to investors that no fundamental policy shift had occurred.

Ditto for press conference number three. When asked a question about the deficit, he pivoted once again to "the core of his economic philosophy":

And part of the charge to my economic team is to find areas where we can get a twofer, where we're getting both a short-term stimulus and we're also laying the groundwork for long-term economic growth.

For example, during my campaign I talked about the need to provide a tax cut to 95 percent of workers. Now, for us to get that tax cut in place, that is going to put money into the pockets of the middle class and will help them in spending for their basic needs. That can help the economy. The sooner we do that, the better.

That will also, though, restore some balance to our tax code over the long term. So that's an example of where the immediate needs of the economy and the long-term concerns that we have are not necessarily incompatible.

Let's perform a little more rhetorical algebra. What does "restore balance to our tax code" signify? It signifies a tax rate for the bottom half that is roughly zero (or less), and a tax rate for the top earners that is somewhere in the neighborhood of 50 percent all in. How is that balance? Because the baseline Obama's using is not actual, absolute tax rates, but recent changes in rates. In other words, if Bush took the top rate down from 40 percent to 35 percent, it would be seen as "giving" money to the wealthy. The hated wealthy have been given too much in the eyes of the Left, so "balance" must be maintained. Like young Anakin Skywalker, Obama is "the Chosen One" who has been sent to restore the balance of the universe.

Please excuse the length of this section, but it is very important that you learn to discern the structure of the new president's thoughts; your success as an investor is dependent on your mastery of this skill. It is in the nature of gradualist social-ism to appear calm and nonthreatening to the business com-munity. This was true a century ago when very few people were investors, and it is truer now that most of us are. It is essential to be able to tell the difference between a genuine policy shift to the center and a counterfeit one.

I want you to be especially careful about retail investing. Not only does trickle-up economics fail to grow the economy in general, but it has little lasting impact even on retail spend-ing. That's because human beings are rational creatures when it comes to their economic decisions (if not their voting ones). Their spending patterns conform largely to their expectations of their long-term income prospects. In other words, we basi-cally decide what class we're in, and then spend accordingly. We may time things a little differently on occasion, waiting for prices to drop in a deflationary cycle or holding off on some purchases during a panic. But then we return to baseline. Any stimulus large enough to get us to the store will at most just cause the local Walmart to staff up for a couple of months with temps, who will then be laid off once the checks are spent. Don't make a long-term bet on retail stocks in response to a stimulus plan.

## Bail 'Em and Nail 'Em

I once debated Jared Bernstein when he was working for a union-funded think tank. Now he is a key player in the Obama administration and chief economist for the vice president. Bern-stein was advocating vast increases in the regulatory powers of the state over capital markets and I was arguing against them. At one point Jared loudly exclaimed, "If you can bail 'em, you can nail 'em!" How revelatory: you "can nail 'em." In other words, it is a given that business should be nailed by the Left; the bailouts provide the justification for a goal already established before subsidies are contemplated.

The numerous and expensive bailouts initiated under the Bush administration have provided ample material that the Left has used to micromanage, bully, and in some cases to outright nationalize large swaths of American business.

Obama and the Left have a complicated relationship with business bailouts, which it is very important for you as an investor to understand.

Let's look now at Obama's rhetorical approach to business subsidies. We've already looked at Obama's first press conference after the election. You've seen that his first priority was a massive system of transfer payments from top earners to consumers. What was his second priority?

> Second, we have to address the spreading impact of the financial crisis on the other sectors of our economy—small businesses that are struggling to meet their payrolls and finance their holiday inventories, and state and municipal governments facing devastating budget cuts and tax increases. . . . The news coming out of the auto industry this week reminds us of the hardship it faces—hardship that goes far beyond individual auto companies to the countless suppliers, small businesses, and communities throughout our nation who depend on a vibrant American auto industry. The auto industry is the backbone of American manufacturing and a critical part of our attempt to reduce our dependence on foreign oil.
>
> I would like to see the administration do everything it can to accelerate the retooling assistance that Congress

has already enacted. In addition, I have made it a high priority for my transition team to work on additional policy options to help the auto industry adjust, weather the financial crisis, and succeed in producing fuel-efficient cars here in the United States of America.

Note, please, the brilliant pivot from small business to the auto industry. I've debated a number of Obama proxies, and each of them has mimicked the same tactic: bailing out large, politically favored corporations is done really for the sake of small business, we're told, because so many small businesses depend on the bailee. That talking point came from the top down; from Obama to proxy, and not vice versa.

This is, of course, an absurd argument. The government takes money from every small business in the country with more than $250,000 in annual profit and transfers it directly to, for example, the UAW (bypassing the shareholders and upper management). Then this transfer is rationalized on the basis that a small fraction of small businesses are directly dependent on the beneficiary. This is an abuse of sound economics. The reasoning is utterly fallacious, but the propaganda is brilliant. Obama gets to rescue a dinosaur industry, repay his union constituency, and frame it as a small business bailout, all at the same time.

Note also the social engineering aspect of these bailouts. Auto subsidies are contingent on a green agenda. If you take the money, the Big Three are told, you must manufacture the kind of cars we want you to manufacture, not the kind of cars that consumers want you to manufacture. Whom will this benefit? A very wealthy network of private equity players who invest early in politically favored technology projects, such as hydrogen fuel cells, hybrid vehicles, and all of the input mechanisms and processes that precede them. These people have already become extremely wealthy on the government's dime. They will become even more so under Obama.

The Left likes to characterize classical supply-side economics as trickle-down economics, but this labeling is wrong. Pumping capital from self-made entrepreneurs into giant auto companies and already well funded green welfare queens on the thin justification that it will, eventually, help consumers spend and workers work is the true instance of trickle-down economics.

## No Newt

"Congress to the rescue!" is hardly a confidence-inspiring battle cry. Yet many commentators are shouting it from the rooftops anyway. In this scenario the Republican midterm electoral gains dramatically change the correlation of political forces and rescue us from antigrowth policies. In the best-case version of this scenario, the newly resurgent House GOP reverses the leftward drift of the past several years. In the worst-case version of this sunny scenario, the GOP brings the system to a point of gridlock, the "sweet spot" for economic growth.

But neither congressional reversal nor even congressional gridlock is realistic.

First of all, reversal of the current policy direction is a political pipe dream. Of course, droves of Republican bes and wannabes flooded the airwaves after the passage of national health care vowing repeal, but who were they kidding? All that was much more of a bid for air time than a serious program. It will take a supermajority of Congress to overcome the inevitable presidential veto that would be associated with health care reversal. Likewise for stimulus spending programs, credit card company regulations, and all the rest of it. Whatever Obama fought hard to pass, he will fight doubly hard to preserve.

The same rules apply for any of the myriad scheduled tax hikes of 2011. President Bush caved in to Democratic members of Congress in 2003 and made his tax cut program temporary. He scheduled most of it to sunset in 2011. This is the law. Congress was not required to pass these tax hikes; they are automatic. Therefore, the legislative approach to stopping a rise in taxes involves a positive action of Congress, one that would almost certainly be blocked by a presidential veto. It takes two-thirds of the members of Congress to overcome a presidential veto. Tax hikes are safe. End of story.

The veto power is a legitimate grant of authority under Article II of the U.S. Constitution. But what about the arrogation of powers not specifically enumerated in that article? This has become a serious issue under President Obama, who has stretched the assumed powers of the president beyond all historical recognition. He has announced strange new uses of his expenditure authority, expanding it into a tool of policy and not just purchasing. The federal government is the largest single consuming entity in America, and if it decides, as it has, to place its thumb on the scale, favoring suppliers who comply with practices approved by labor unions and their political allies, it has enormous consequences for businesses whose practices are deemed not to be socially beneficial.

More disturbing is the practice of vague congressional "enabling legislation," which leaves nearly all specific matters to executive branch rule–making authorities. The health care bill, for example, is more like a 2,900–page Zip file, which has been downloaded into the systems of the Health and Human Services Department and the Internal Revenue Service and the Labor Department, where it will unzip into tens of thousands of individual pages of mandates, each one written by someone intensely hostile to a market-based health care system.

Similar approaches are being taken toward areas that have not received full congressional support, such as a "cap and trade" system of carbon rationing. The EPA has asserted the authority to regulate carbon dioxide (the gas that is exhaled by every single member of the animal kingdom) as a pollutant. Bizarrely innovative legal strategies have been concocted that allow regulation of all hydrocarbon consumption (which constitutes nearly all energy in the United States) on the basis of the Endangered Species Act. Since polar bears are registered as endangered, and government-run panels assert a link between carbon emissions, global temperatures, and alleged loss of polar ice, then our entire economy can be tethered for the sake of protecting the bears.

These tactics are currently being used to invade nearly every area of American economic life, from anti-sprawl transportation funding plans to politically directed credit markets. In the 1980s, the Reagan administration had a motto: "Personnel is policy." Unfortunately, Obama seems to know that, too.

# CHAPTER TWO

# Obamanomics 101

It is very important for you to understand President Obama's basic model of the economy. For him, business enterprises are parasitical entities. Business doesn't serve the masses; businesses are served by the masses who buy the products. Consumers are seen as the providers of financial capital, not investors. Mass consumption is the center of the economic story.

Social capital is created by people who work in the government and nonprofit sectors. Nurses, teachers, social workers, and community organizers are the center of the cultural story.

Businesses are to be subordinated to the consumer and the organizer.

Mrs. Obama bragged during the campaign that she and Barack had not gone into business to make a lot of money. He had become a community organizer, and she had gone to work in health care.

He shares his wife's philosophy. In his first autobiography, he describes his very brief postgraduation stint in the business sector as "like a spy behind enemy lines." Business is the enemy because, in his mind, business consumes resources. Large accumulations of money can be found on Wall Street, but what does it produce? Nothing that you can see. An inner-city pastor gathers a visible crowd; so does a community organizer. You can see the people, the fervor on their faces. You can count their votes. This is real. The crowd is real. The bigger the crowd, the more real it is. Markets are not visible, therefore they are not real. This is Obama's moral universe.

So in the center of his moral universe is the politically organized community, not the economy.

But the crowd is in the center of his economic model, as well, not just his political model. The Left tends to invert the role of the consumer and the producer. Since businesses are looking for customers, the Left mistakenly comes to believe that consumers are the creators of wealth. Now, of course, you understand that in our role as productive workers, we ordinary citizens are the creators of wealth. When we take our paychecks and then turn around and buy things with them, we become consumers. We must first produce, and then consume. There is only one place that I can think of where "consumption" precedes "production"—the dictionary!

Saint Paul said, "If a man will not work, neither will he eat." Saint Paul was not a leftist, though. The Left inverts this basic economic cycle. For them, the consumer is the origin of wealth. If he stops consuming, he must be stimulated. The printing press must be revved up, and the resulting dollars must be dropped from helicopters to the masses. Money must be taken from the selfish savers of the economy (see the moral inversion again?) and transferred to mass consumers. But since the bottom half of America basically pays no federal income taxes, how, then, can 95 percent of Americans be given a tax cut? By calling a transfer payment a tax cut, that's how.

But it is of the utmost importance that you understand that this redistribution regime is not just a vote-buying exercise. It is an attempt at a prosperity-buying exercise, as well. Mass movements are at the heart of both left-wing and right-wing populism. The organized mass of citizens is the key to political power, and the organized mass of spenders is the key to economic recovery. Unfortunately for us, in the real world, only the former strategy works, not the latter one. You can win elections from time to time with mass populism, but you cannot grow wealth that way.

When politicians rail against trickle-down economics, they are really railing against markets, and by extension, investors themselves. They are setting the stage for mass redistribution. And they mischaracterize those of us who believe in a free society, because we do not advocate trickle-down economics, nor trickle-up economics. We advocate allowing wealth creators at whatever level to keep all of their wealth, except the small amount needed to run basic government services. In fact, as usual, the Left is guilty of the very accusation that they level against their enemies. Obama and company are the real practitioners of coercive trickle-down economics.

Trickle-down economics relies on taxpayer subsidies to business. The government takes taxes from all and pumps the money to the top of the economic pyramid, in the mistaken belief that it will trickle down to the people. Trickle-up economics taxes all and pumps the money to the bottom, in the mistaken belief that it will trickle up to the top.

Classical economists believe that wealth should be left for the most part with the people who created it in the first place.

They knew enough to produce that wealth, and if we leave it with them, we believe that they will produce more of it. We don't want to be trickled on at all. So, if you have a picture in your head that shows a divide in the policy road, the left side of which is labeled "trickle-up economics" and the right side of which is labeled "trickle-down economics," throw that picture away. Replace it with this one: a fork in the road in which one road is labeled "central planning" and the other is labeled "free markets." The central planning road has sections labeled "trickle up" and "trickle down" to signify the policies that subsidize politically favored groups, some at the top (for example, alternative-energy venture capital funds) and some at the bottom (for example, autoworkers). The other road is filled with houses and businesses of various sizes, and each keeps the lion's share of its labors—no trickling. Trickling implies a pump; it treats economics as a giant problem in hydraulic engineering. The central planner can pump money up to the commanding heights of industry, or down to the teeming masses, but he is the engineer who determines the course of the water. Not surprisingly, the most influential propagandist of Keynesian central planning (other than Keynes himself) was A. W. Phillips, known for the Phillips Curve. Before he studied economics, he was an engineer. For his doctoral work in Keynesian theory, he produced not a paper, but a machine—a giant economic forecasting machine based on water flow, complete with tanks and pumps representing pools of capital and their spending flows. Phillips laid the groundwork for the widespread adoption of central planning throughout the English-speaking world. He helped shift our view of human nature away from the view that we are independent, intelligent, and (above all) active beings with our own dignity, toward the view that we are parts of classes, inert and in need of massive fiscal and monetary pumps to move us from one place to another. The only debate left for the central planner was "when to pump up" and "when to pump down."

Obama sees the world in exactly this way: pump up to auto manufacturers and ethanol merchants, pump down to transfer payment recipients. If that doesn't work, place the pumps elsewhere and try again. If $1 trillion doesn't do the job, add another trillion, and another after that.

This model has been tried before, most recently in Japan since the 1990s. The results are very instructive.

# CHAPTER THREE

# Applied Obamanomics

## The Japanese Ghost Economy

*"Wizards can leave an imprint of themselves upon the earth, to walk palely where their living selves once trod," said Nick miserably. "But very few wizards choose that path."*

*"Why not?" said Harry. "Anyway—it doesn't matter—Sirius won't care if it's unusual, he'll come back, I know he will!". . .*

*"He will not come back," repeated Nick quietly. "He will have . . . gone on."*

*"What d'you mean, 'gone on'?" said Harry quickly. "Gone on where? Listen—what happens when you die, anyway? Where do you go? Why doesn't everyone come back? Why isn't this place full of ghosts? Why—?"*

*"I cannot answer," said Nick.*

*"You're dead, aren't you?" said Harry exasperatedly. "Who can answer better than you?"*

*"I was afraid of death," said Nick. "I chose to remain behind. I sometimes wonder whether I oughtn't to have . . . well, that is*

*neither here nor there . . . In fact, I am neither here nor there . . ."*
*He gave a small sad chuckle. "I know nothing of the secrets of*
*death, Harry, for I chose my feeble imitation of life instead."*

Harry's godfather, Sirius Black, had just been murdered. Unable to accept the finality of his loss, Harry asked the ghost, Sir Nicholas, about how he had come back. But he had not come back; Sir Nicholas had never gone on in the first place. He had chosen "to walk palely" on the earth, rather than to risk what may lie ahead.

I know it is odd to use a passage from a children's novel to illustrate a point about economic stagnation. It shouldn't be. I wish more financial commentators would use literature (pop or classical) to illustrate their points. It makes sense to do so, because behind all of the statistics and technical fog, economics is really about human nature, and its tendency toward either arrogance or anxiety. What stands behind the great Japanese stagnation and the soft socialism that has dominated western Europe for most of the postwar period is a very human characteristic—the inability to accept risk. This is the nature of all societies, but much more so of traumatized societies, as it is the nature of traumatized persons. They seek security. They try to take the risk out of life. Like the wizards in the world of Harry Potter who choose to leave a vague imprint of themselves in the world in order to avoid the discovery of what lies beyond, they will choose a half life over a full and risky one. Much of the Order of the Phoenix is about risk and security. The leader of the government, Cornelius Fudge, a proxy for Neville Chamberlain, deals with unpleasant news by simply shouting it down. There is no threat. The old ways of war are over. Wizard-kind faces no existential threat. Anyone who says otherwise is lying. Harry and his friends embrace the unpleasant truth, and take the ultimate risk, laying their lives on the line to save their friends. The aforementioned Sirius Black chooses risk again and again to support his godson Harry. He ends up dying for that. Sir Nicholas knows that a man who takes risks like that will not deprive himself of the knowledge of what lies behind the veil in exchange for a vague, eternal drift wherein nothing ever really is lost—or gained.

Before we get into the policy details, I wanted to give you this picture of the psychology behind the stagnant economies of Japan and Western Europe. Imagine them as ghost economies palely walking through the years.

The Japanese government tried to control the economy. They had mistakenly believed that the government could provide growth through stimulus. The result was that they were neither here nor there. No big rallies, no big recessions, just wandering sideways across the stock ticker. Western Europe chose the same fate. The eminent historian Paul Johnson once told me that Europe had simply given up its responsibility to preserve itself, because it was frightened—frightened by World War I, a trauma that it had not believed was possible—frightened by World War II, a repetition of something about which they had vowed to themselves "never again," and the long twilight existential threat of the cold war, from which they were (for a third time) rescued by the United States. Europe almost destroyed itself three times in the past century and was rescued three times by a power for whom it has never really had any respect. This is very hard on a people.

Add the side effects of war and disruption, hyperinflation, deflation, unemployment, depression, and you get electorates with a desire for nothing but rest and security from womb to tomb. This requires an extensive welfare state, and an extensive welfare state requires high taxes, and high taxes slow economic growth.

## Gradual Nationalization

Many commentators failed to see the ferocity with which the administration would pursue its national health care objectives.

They missed the almost mystical and eschatological awe in which the Left holds the de-privatization of the health sector. Obama's base measured him against Clinton on one issue more than any other—health care nationalization. The advocates of a unified national health service felt that somehow during the early '90s they had been robbed of something to which they were entitled. They blamed the insurance companies and the pharmaceutical companies who "spent millions of dollars" on the "Harry and Louise" ads that allegedly scuttled the dream of free health care for everyone.

This narrative was nearly always repeated with indignation and with suggestive overtones that something sinister had been done by the coalition that defeated the plan. How dare the health care industry object to wholesale reorganization of one-seventh of the economy that they operate every day with their own knowledge, skills, and capital? How dare they make their case to the public? How dare they purchase air time to rebut the pro-nationalization case that was being made for free every day on the news? How dare they exercise their constitutional right to "petition the government for a redress of grievances" by hiring professional government and public relations specialists to make their case to the Congress about the legislative approach?

That was the attitude then, and that attitude appeared again, on steroids (available with no co-pay), under the Obama administration. Since the early 1990s, the rights of businesses to make their case to the government and directly to the public have been severely curtailed through much more restrictive campaign finance regulations, only a small portion of which have for the time being been struck down by the Supreme Court. In addition, the level of intimidation against media that do not toe the line has risen dramatically.

The Left could not have thrown in the towel in their fight to take the commanding heights of American health care. The Obama transition team had analyzed the Clinton health care case study very carefully. They came to different conclusions than did many Clinton insiders.

The view of the Clinton team can be summarized as follows: The American political system has a limited appetite for large changes. It can only digest one or two big morsels at a time. Clinton asked for a big stimulus package, a modest tax increase, and a wholesale restructuring of health delivery all at the same time. The system couldn't handle all that, hence the legislative defeat of HillaryCare and the electoral defeat of the Democratic leaders of Congress in 1994.

> The politics were also very complicated, and I thought Lloyd Bentsen, who had been the savvy chairman of the Senate Finance Committee before becoming Treasury Secretary, made a lot of sense when he said that the President's deficit reduction plan and health care reform were simply too much for our political system to process at one time.
>
> —ROBERT RUBIN, *In an Uncertain World*

Although most of the general public (who do not spend their lives studying the HillaryCare debacle) did not notice the sound of it, Obama sent out a none-too-subtle dog whistle to the Clinton moderates and other Democratic policy insiders from the very beginning of his administration:

Now, there are some who question the scale of our ambitions—who suggest that our system cannot tolerate too many big plans. Their memories are short. For they have forgotten what this country has already done; what free men and women can achieve when imagination is joined to common purpose, and necessity to courage.

What the cynics fail to understand is that the ground has shifted beneath them—that the stale political arguments that have consumed us for so long no longer apply.

The question we ask today is not whether our government is too big or too small, but whether it works—whether it helps families find jobs at a decent wage, care they can afford, a retirement that is dignified. Where the answer is yes, we intend to move forward.

In other words:

Clinton, Bentsen, and Rubin were wrong when they raised cautions about going too far too fast. They went too slow and not far enough. They lacked ambition. I, President Obama, do not. I will succeed where they failed. All who oppose me are "cynics" with "stale arguments" who have had the ground shifted out from under them without even knowing it. I want this bad enough to horse-trade away other public programs in order to get enough moderates on board to realize my historical legacy. The other Democratic presidents, Roosevelt, Truman, Johnson, Carter, and Clinton, tried and failed. I, Obama, will succeed.

In order to accomplish a very rapid pace of change, Obama tended to govern more from the White House itself than from the cabinet posts that are spread throughout D.C. Physical proximity to Obama tends to figuratively determine proximity to power. Former White House special advisor Karl Rove has described the feng shui of power in the Obama staff structure:

Many Americans may assume that the president's entire staff is in the West Wing. It's not. The West Wing is actually a very small place, so the vast number of people who work "at the White House" actually have offices across the street at the Eisenhower Executive Office Building (EEOB).

Under Mr. Obama, the political director won't be in the EEOB, where other presidents have placed him. He'll occupy a West Wing office usually given to the head of presidential personnel. That's a sign of the importance of politics for Team Obama. . . .

Another first to have a West Wing office is the incoming secretary of Health and Human Services, Tom Daschle. Once sworn in, he will be the first domestic cabinet secretary to have a desk in the most coveted office space in government—to use in his other job as director of the White House Office of Health Reform.

This dual role centralizes policy-making inside the White House because it allows Mr. Daschle to displace the Domestic Policy Council and the National Economic Council on developing health-care policy.

—KARL ROVE, "THE OBAMA WHITE HOUSE MAY
BE A CROWDED MESS," *Wall Street Journal*

Any clearheaded observer of Washington knew the moment Obama announced the appointment of Daschle as HHS head that the president was not in any way moderating his policy objectives on health care. Daschle eventually was forced to withdraw his name in one of the many Obama nominee tax-evasion scandals. But just because Daschle is out doesn't mean that the Daschle playbook departed with him. Daschle, the former head of the Senate Democrats, had used his retirement to create a book-length game plan on how to ram a universal health care system through a resistant political culture. This is something that a number of the top Obama advisors in the West Wing have in common: a history of penning books and articles that entirely skip the policy debate and go right to the power politics. They are utterly devoid of any sense of self-doubt about the wisdom of overriding the private system. Team Obama is right: The people who currently operate the health care system are wrong. Team Obama needs to be in charge, now.

"How do we get it done?" That's the only question they asked of themselves.

They got it done by isolating the health care industry from the other sectors of industry. Large corporations are burdened with high health care costs, due to excessive government mandates, inefficient tax code treatment, and a blizzard of lawsuit abuse. The administration attracted corporate America to support nationalization by the promise of off-loading their health care costs onto the general public. This divides the business coalition between those businesses that are saddled with unusually high health care costs—unionized manufacturers, for instance—and those for whom health care is a relatively small share of payroll—for example, financial services firms and companies that use a lot of subcontractors. There were many press availabilities featuring middle-aged men in business suits standing next to the president, while the latter proclaims that "the business community is on board with fundamental change in the way we deliver health care in this country, except for a few holdouts who cynically appeal to our fears and not our hopes . . . yada, yada, yada."

No stone was left unturned, no vote left unpurchased, no family member left without a federal judgeship, no pork left unladled until it was done. The legislative sausage factory ground out its product in such an unseemly way that one wonders how long it will be before actual sausage factories begin to object to the oft-repeated comparisons to Congress. And, finally, it was done.

But what, exactly, was done?

The legislation has set up an alternate, government-provided health care financing system. It is funded by numerous taxes that are gradually being imposed on businesses that do not provide health care to their employees above a certain minimum level of coverage, health insurance companies themselves, high-income investors, medical device manufacturers, and sundry other political scapegoats. The government has arrogated the right to determine what constitutes a certain minimal level of coverage. Purchase less than the minimum for yourself, and you'll be fined. Purchase less than that for your employees, and you'll be fined some more.

Conspicuously missing is the typical small business exemption; there will only be a "smallest" business exemption. Businesses of fifty employees and under will not be subject to the tax penalty for now. The rarest form of business in America will quickly become businesses with fifty-one employees. If you have fifty employees and you think you might be able to expand and add a few more people, think again. Better to make do with what you have, or launch the new product as an entirely separate business.

The parallel health care system, therefore, is voluntary in terms of participation, but not voluntary in terms of financing. The private sector is being forced to subsidize the public sector with which it is competing. The greater the number of benefits in the public sector, the greater the costs that are to be imposed on the private sector. The idea is that there should be a gradual, but inevitable, migration of people from the cost-bearing private system to the benefit-conferring public one.

This is a gradual form of health care nationalization. It is the template not just for the health care sector but for the energy sector as well, and perhaps for the banking sector. In each case the old, private system will be placed under more and more restrictive mandates. The new regulatory regime that intends to rule our health, energy, and financial sectors is immensely complex to begin with and also contains contradictory elements. Therefore, it is literally impossible to fully obey. Being on the right side of the law, as a result, is a matter of being on the right side of the politicians, who can then decide which mandates to ignore and which to enforce.

For example, as I write, members of Congress are ordering banks to lend more freely. At the same time, members of the bureaucracy that has oversight of the banks are telling the banks to increase their capital. So, should the bankers lend out more money as Congress commands? Or should they hold the money in reserves as a capital cushion? They cannot do both things with the same dollar.

Here is another example. Shortly before the chairman of General Motors, Rick Wagoner, was forced out at the request of the administration, that same administration issued a written critique of Mr. Wagoner's plan to save the company. One section of the report said that the company had not yet developed a plan that would lead to sufficient profit to lead to viability. But another section of the report faulted the automaker for being insufficiently bold in moving toward more fuel-efficient cars. The problem is that the verboten larger cars are far more profitable than the beloved green ones. So what is a CEO to do, follow the administration's command to make shareholders more money, or follow the administration's command to make products more green?

With the cost of the new nationally approved health, energy, financial, and other sectors being borne by the "old" nationally shunned private versions, the private versions will lose market share to their new and improved public doppelgangers. This is the Obama playbook. We don't know whether it will work in the long run or if, instead, the American people are able to see the pattern and elect representatives who will put a stop to it. But we do know with a considerable degree of confidence what the policy drift will look like over the next few years, and smart investors should be prepared for it.


## How Bad Could Things Get?

Let's start with some iron laws of human economic life: Wage and price controls cause gluts and shortages.

Price floors cause gluts.

Price ceilings, on the other hand, cause shortages.

If we enter into a period of sustained inflation, price ceilings become plausible. After all, the Nixon-era wage and price controls were launched in response to an inflation rate of less than 5 percent. The Obama administration is guilty of not having learned from the Nixon experience how terribly destructive price controls are. Exhibit 1 in defense of this accusation is that the health care bill creates a national premium-setting board for private health care providers. Exhibit 2 in defense of the accusation is that the credit card bill also contains strong elements of price control.

To understand the pattern of inflation, control, and shortage, let's look at the sector that has most often been subjected to it: food.

If the state forbids farmers from selling food at the market price, then the farmers are less willing to sell it. Consumers will demand more food at the cheaper price, but they will have more trouble finding it. If the market distortions are large enough, none will be found. When we are free, the price rises to a level at which consumers are willing to buy and producers are willing to sell. When we're not free, the transaction does not occur. This is why food shortages are so extremely common under socialist regimes. This is why statist dictators historically have railed against peasant farmers allegedly hoarding food; because farmers don't want to sell their goods at a loss.

Anyone who wants to understand why populist socialist regimes so often turn toward violent episodes of peasant extermination need only understand this simple political economic dynamic: price ceilings cause shortages. The planners are almost never willing to take responsibility for the disruptive effects of their plans, and so "greed" and "hoarding" are blamed. The answer to hoarding is some form of forcible redistribution of the resource in question; in this case, food. Since people resist—either rhetorically or more stringently—the forced confiscation of their property, socialist regimes tend to enforce their diktats rhetorically *and* more stringently.

This dynamic was described most powerfully by the Nobel Prize–winning economist Friedrich Hayek in his book *The Road to Serfdom*. Hayek argued that the allegedly humane socialist regimes that had opposed Hitler would themselves be pulled in the direction of dictatorship. This would occur, according to Hayek, because interventions cause crises. Since it is rare for someone with power to acknowledge the ill effects of his commands, the governing classes generally try to solve the intervention-triggered crises with another intervention. The "corrective" intervention causes another crisis and so another intervention is launched. Since government interventions are by their very nature distortion creators, the problems are not solved, and the state continues to grow. Such large states work on the basis of unified national purpose, and so dissent must be crushed one way or another.

Has Hayek's thesis been borne out by subsequent history? Since the book was published in 1945, a pattern similar to that of Hayek's thesis has emerged in some countries, but not in all. Joshua Muravchik, in his definitive history of socialism, *Heaven on Earth*, modified Hayek in light of a fuller reading of history. Soft socialist countries do tend to turn toward harder socialism. First they cajole, then they regulate, and eventually they nationalize large swaths of the private sector. The true owners of the businesses resist: they withdraw capital, withdraw their labors, and sometimes even withdraw themselves and their families. One way or another, they go on strike. This, according to Muravchik, is the moment of truth for the socialist ruler. In many cases, such as British Labour socialism after World War II, the rulers pull back. Having hit a resistance point, they stop pushing. They consolidate some gains in state power, but not all. They declare that the people are "not yet ready" for truly progressive government and pledge their commitment to further educate the people in the principles of the new economics. Over time, the commanded and controlled sectors of the economy come into public disrepute, and a Thatcher arises and denationalizes the industry in question.

But sometimes things don't work out quite so well. Sometimes the leader, driven by his narcissistic greed for power, pushes harder. He activates and coordinates domestic pressure groups and opinion-molding institutions to demonize the resistant parties. His willing reputation-executioners launch print and broadcast barrages against the "old guard," the "holdouts," and the "reactionaries." Once such a barrage of hate is unleashed, it is difficult to limit it to rhetoric. After all, who can blame the people for hating the supposed enemies of progress and human betterment?

It generally doesn't start as an overt government action, but rather as a government of malign neglect of vigilantism. If unidentified hordes of angry young people smash the windows of Jewish vendors in 1930s Germany (or of bankers in modern Britain and America), then nothing is done. Union violence remains technically illegal, but broadly tolerated.

How *might* this scenario play out in a modern American context? Don't expect to see armed soldiers dragging newspaper editors out of their homes at midnight. That is sooo 1930s. Expect something more like modern Central American populist leftism: intimidation, but not brutal suppression. Expect a blurring of the distinction between assault and "protest." Conservative events will be disrupted, in some cases so severely that they will be unable to be completed. Worship services will be interrupted. People who are not on board will be verbally assaulted by professional insulters like Jon Stewart and Stephen Colbert in the foulest possible terms. Leftist events, however, will be guarded and controlled; *those* demonstrators will be handled brutally.

Under this scenario, the media would be intimidated in subtler ways. Under the Sandinistas, opposition groups were technically permitted to publish their newspapers; they just couldn't procure the paper to print them on. You can speak out against Chavez on a street corner, but it's almost impossible for his opponents to operate TV stations. You can speak out as a private citizen against the drift toward statism, but expect to be called into meetings with your employers, who are themselves having their arms twisted by the government. In an environment in which government is growing beyond its traditional bounds, nearly everyone is working—in one way or another—for someone who is directly dependent on the goodwill of government. This model is not entirely alien to American culture: political machines have operated this way for many years. It is rare nowadays, but not entirely absent. This type of thuggish politics is still routinely practiced in Chicago, from whence our current president hails.

During the high-water-mark period of bailout nation, former Clinton labor secretary Robert Reich ran ads financed by the Service Employees International Union in which he called upon the government to fire the CEO of Bank of America because he opposed union card check legislation. Reich served under Clinton and serves as an advisor to Obama. That is already intimidation. Even if the president never fired Ken Lewis, Lewis knew that the president could, and that at least one of the president's advisors had suggested that he should, and that the president had already fired the CEO of GM, partly for his failure to tow the line on environmental policy. You don't have to wait until the government actually deposes a CEO before you call it intimidation; by the time the threat has been raised, intimidation has already occurred. This is, in fact, the point of the threat: the most effective intimidators almost never have to get beyond the threat stage.

Media conglomerates have already been feeling the pressure. CNBC, for which I do some work, was owned by GE, which does work with the federal government. The network executives convened a meeting with hosts and producers to discuss their concerns about whether the station has done too much "Obama bashing." The question is not whether America will move at all toward the Chavez model (we have already done that); I think the question is how far in that direction we will go.

It goes without saying that this political climate would produce a much more destructive economic climate than the one I've presented in much of this book. It is a twentieth-century myth that centrally planned autarchies are efficiently run—that they offer no freedom, but at least the trains run on time. The suppression of human rights is not the price that the citizens pay for efficiency, as the myth suggests. The suppression of human rights is the state's solution to the problem of inefficiency. It is precisely because the trains arrive late, and not loaded with food and clothing in command-and-control economies, that there is unrest. Rather than release their hold on the flow of goods and services, autocrats tighten their hold on the people.

Militarism is part of this phenomenon, as well. Again, the myth is wrong: War mobilization does not lead to greater efficiencies in the production of consumer goods and services. If it did, large-scale wars would be times of material abundance rather than rations and victory gardens. War is not the solution to the problem of domestic production scarcity; it is the solution to the problem of domestic *dissatisfaction* with production scarcity. War is a distraction from the failure of the state planners. It is a means of acquiring resources from neighboring countries when the aggressor country lacks the capacity to create sufficient wealth on its own.

The full-blown Chavez scenario is not likely. The United States has a far stronger tradition of resistance to supra-legal government encroachments than any nation in the world. We have a slim majority of citizens and a significant majority of voters who are members of the investor class. Although most of the print and broadcast media outlets favor statist solutions to economic problems, there is a very vibrant set of voices on talk radio, cable news, and the Internet who are highly resistant to left-wing autocratic populism. The recent spate of Tea Parties is a testament to this fact. I say this not in the hope that President Obama is in his heart unwilling to suppress his political enemies. I think he has been so steeped in the ideologies of power through Saul Alinsky–inspired community activism, and racialist forms of liberation theology, that in times of political crisis he may well default to his baseline. I say it not in the hope that he will change his mind; history shows few examples of very highly ambitious men in positions of great power who respond to resistance with conciliation. I say it in the hope that America will not follow a man who follows that direction. I don't trust the president not to be Chavez, but I trust the people of America not to be Venezuelans.

# CHAPTER FOUR

# You Are Here

## That '70s Show

Let's leave aside speculation about how bad things might get in favor of observations about how bad they already are. Historically, nations that have embarked on the social democrat, welfare state path have tried to overcome stagnation with the printing press. But the Nixon/Ford/Carter Keynesian episode of the 1970s taught anyone who was willing to listen that the economic downer of central planning cannot be countered with the economic upper of loose money. You can't print your way into prosperity; you can only print your way into inflation.

The central planners have tended to favor monetary policy instead of tax policy as a means of stimulating growth. Their view is that capitalism is prone to periodic imbalances of underspending. They believe that free economies tend to create great concentrations of wealth, and that the wealthy beneficiaries of capitalism are given to hoarding their assets in large pools of idle capital. The rich get richer, and clutch it in their greedy talons. The poor get poorer and, though willing to spend, don't have enough money to produce the aggregate demand that the economy needs.

The solution lies, the planners tell us, in the hands of the central bankers. They can "stimulate" demand by creating more money. More dollars circulating around the economy means each dollar is falling in value. Each dollar buys less and less in the marketplace, or to put it conversely, each item in the market costs more. This "inflation tax" punishes savers and rewards spenders. People buy things now instead of later, because they'll cost more later than they do now. Consumer spending rises, giving the temporary impression of prosperity, but the price of the items rises at least as quickly as income, so people spend more but don't have more. Businesses put all of their efforts into meeting that short-term demand spike, and no new efforts into capital upgrades. There is little capital available for them anyway, because savers are hesitant to lend, demanding higher interest rates to compensate them for the risk of inflation. Consequently, productivity rates fall.

This is what happened to us in the 1970s. We got two things at the same time that the arbiters of economic opinion told us could not simultaneously exist in the economy: stagnation and inflation. The Keynesian model told us that we could get relief from high inflation by stimulating the economy with easy money. We did not. In the end, Milton Friedman turned out to be correct that "inflation is always and everywhere a monetary phenomenon." Prices are a ratio between dollars and goods. If you increase dollars without increasing goods, you don't get higher wealth, you just get higher prices.

The data now point toward a 1970s-style stagflation scenario over any of the other scenarios currently under consideration. Obama has shown no evidence of a "conversion" from the central planning to the pro-growth model as of this writing, and congressional Republicans have shown little ability to dissuade him. In fact, the president seems to interpret each new phase of the crisis as a call to "do more" rather than less. The American political culture seems to have an extremely low pain tolerance when it comes to unemployment and recessions, and is willing to make unprecedented tax and spending bets in order to avoid even normal levels of recessionary pain. This means that the pressure on the Federal Reserve's Open Market Committee (which actually makes the decisions regarding monetary policy) will continue to be enormous. As long as there is the least whiff of hard times in the air, and there will be for the foreseeable future, Mr. Bernanke will continue to avoid monetary tightening like the plague. The problem is that the plague may have already arrived, and it has come in the form of inflation. With three Obama appointments to his board, Mr. Bernanke will find himself unable to get the votes for Fed tightening, even if he wanted them.

Fortunately (for the free-market investor, not for the country) we know the kind of market conditions this policy mix tends to create. Bondholders find themselves in the punishment seat. Anyone owning conventional treasury or corporate fixed-income securities will feel like he's being waterboarded. Stockholders have moments of ecstasy (when the easy money hits the street) and agony (when raw materials prices kill corporate profits) and torment (when they are forced to pay capital gains taxes on merely inflationary gains).

During times of stagflation, some investments hold their value fairly well. Commodities rise in value more quickly than general consumer prices. Real estate tends to do well as a general asset class during inflationary times. Inflation-adjusted bonds, such as Series I Savings Bonds and TIPS

(Treasury Inflation-Protected Securities), are very promising investment vehicles at times like this.

There are even good equity plays, but those have to be chosen carefully. Businesses with a lot of debt tend to do well during inflationary cycles, because they are paying off their creditors with debased currencies. Home builders function well as an equity play when home demand is up. Companies with "pricing power" (the ability to raise prices without suffering proportional decreases in sales) do well. Inflation is a cigarette manufacturer's paradise.

Emerging-market investing becomes much more attractive during times of domestic U.S. inflation. This is true for two reasons. First, emerging-market countries tend to be commodity producers. Second, their assets are denominated in terms of currencies other than the weakening dollar.

To understand how international investing works, you should imagine a very unusual type of casino. In this casino, not only do you gamble when you play the games, but you also gamble when you cash in your chips. You may win at the roulette wheel, but when you take your chips to the cashier, you roll the dice again. Your chips may turn out to be worth more or less than they were when you won them. In this casino, the game of chance applies not just to the official games of chance but to the currency itself.

If I'm right, the dollar will continue to fall in value against better-managed currencies, and this will multiply the investment returns of anyone who is invested in assets denominated in those sounder currencies.

Which currencies are those? For a start, commodity-producing nations are currently less prone to monetary stimulus than other countries. Remember, money creation is generally used in an attempt to goose a flagging economy. This is one of the reasons why currencies of stagnating economies tend to fall in value. Not only are their investments less desirable, but there is a high probability of a misguided attempt to reignite the economy with easy money. Highly taxed, highly regulated resource-consuming developed countries will continue to be plagued with such problems. Hungry, up-and-coming commodity producers will not. Brazil, for example, would tend to do well during a global inflationary commodity boom. This means less temptation to debase the Brazilian real. There are, of course, risks in the emerging markets other than the currency risks.

## Not Giving Credit Where Credit Is Due

The government mandates that led to our global economic crisis have generally not been rescinded. Mark-to-market accounting was, eventually, modified in the spring of 2009, but the original mechanisms of distortion continue to stand. In fact, they are likely to be made even more disruptive. Congressional Democrats are currently pushing for legislation that would extend the Community Reinvestment Act (CRA) to credit unions. Credit union executives are being pressured politically to support this change. Of course, one of the principal reasons credit unions and community banks are financially much stronger than large money-center banks is that they are generally exempt from CRA and its loan mandates.

In addition, there will probably be efforts to extend these regulations to smaller banks. The "fair" housing industry has felt for some time that they were not given nearly enough power to compel minority lending from banks. They resented regulatory exemptions for small banks. They lamented the low level of confidentiality on the information the government was able to demand from banks. They voiced their disappointment with the limited number of tools of punishment the federal government could wield against insufficiently generous banks.

The Bush administration, even with partial congressional majorities, could barely hold off against the rush to ratchet up minority lending mandates in a time of relative financial calm. Now nearly all the political power is in the hands of a former community organizer/fair housing lawyer. The probability that these destructive policies will be intensified greatly exceeds the probability that they will be lessened. This prospect contains enormously pervasive implications for investors and entrepreneurs.

Rich Karlgaard, the publisher of *Forbes* magazine, has seen the implications probably as clearly as anyone:

> Between inflation and a 49% capital gains tax rate, there wasn't much risk capital available in the 1970s. The entrepreneurs bootstrapped their companies. To pay the bills, Larry Ellison and his cohorts wrote software for paying clients during the day; at night they developed what would become the Oracle database. Even during the go-go 1990s, when venture capital flowed like a river, the decade's most successful start-up bootstrapped itself. Google founders Sergey Brin and Larry Page ran up credit cards to buy cheap computers to build the little search engine that could. Outside financing might have killed Google. The founders might have bought gold-plated servers and set themselves on a very expensive path. . . .
>
> Capital is scarce, but smart bootstrappers will prevail.
>
> —RICH KARLGAARD, FORBES.COM,
>
> "BOOTSTRAPPERS RULE"

Karlgaard is right; we have entered (or reentered) a set of conditions that tends to favor bootstrappers over capital-intensive businesses. Unless he is in one of those fields that are politically favored, the guy who needs start-up capital is in trouble. The guy who can make a profit from his first unit sold tends to have the edge.

What do the various types of bootstrappers look like?

They may be owners or managers who have very quick sales cycles. Inventory that sits on the shelves for a long time requires capital. Fast turnover of inventory means less need for credit. Bootstrappers have variable instead of fixed unit costs. In other words, they won't be like pharmaceutical companies that spend a billion dollars to create a drug, then spend a couple of cents for each pill produced. That model requires loads of capital. Bootstrapped products won't take much money to initiate, so they are profitable almost from the beginning.

Software sometimes may constitute an exception to this rule. Software is almost entirely a front-loaded cost business. The money is spent creating the program. After that, the variable cost—that is, the cost of each new unit of production—is minuscule. It takes hundreds of millions of dollars to write an MS Windows upgrade, but almost nothing to put it on a disc.

But small software developers can be bootstrappers, not because they avoid the problem of up-front costs, but because they absorb those costs personally. A programmer can spend his days churning out code for Google, and his evenings churning out code for himself. He can write or modify small applications on his own time, which he can then sell later. Like any other front-loaded business, he needs an investor, but in this case he is his own investor. He builds his business with sweat equity (or at least carpal tunnel equity). That guy can make it in these bootstrapping times.

Sometimes bootstrappers turn their customers into investors. They embark on large projects for which they bill the client in progress. In this sense, the customer is lending the bootstrapper the money that he needs to build the product. This only works when the product is unusual and the customer really needs it (or is an in-law). Otherwise, the customer would just go someplace else to get his widget, or go widgetless entirely.

Bootstrappers also turn their suppliers into investors. They arrange slow payment terms, or sometimes simply refuse to honor normal payment terms. I don't recommend the latter. It's not honest, and in the long run it doesn't work. But suppliers who themselves are desperate to sell products in tough times may agree to extended payment terms. In this way, the start-up borrows from his suppliers, so that he can create products that he can sell to his customers to generate the revenues he needs to turn around and repay his suppliers. If your supplier is desperate enough to go for this, then make sure that he's not so desperate as to be on the verge of going out of business just when you need him. Usually companies are not willing to do this unless they have a lot of cash on hand. Cash on hand is rare during credit crunches but becomes abundant during inflation surges. For entrepreneurs and for investors both, timing is critical in the world of bootstrapping.

## Dis-Integration

Imagine a primitive society, a small village perhaps, in which people produce goods and services and trade them with one another on a voluntary basis. In a situation like this, virtually all of the economic production and trading occurs between people who know one another, who trade face-to-face. And if they don't know one another directly, then they know one another indirectly. Essentially, a small village is, in some sense, an economic extended family. Although there is trading with other villages, this is not the chief means of wealth creation and entrepreneurship.

There would certainly be laws that would enforce the agreements people make with one another, but they would be less sophisticated than what we now know as contract law, in which there is a well-defined set of terms: an offer, an acceptance of that offer, well-established terms of payment—the things we take for granted in our modern civilization whenever we engage in economic activity. In our imaginary village there is a more rudimentary set of laws, but as a simple, practical matter these laws are not the main means of enforcing the agreements. The agreements are enforced by the social pressure that people feel to keep their promises when they're dealing with somebody they know well. This is similar to the social pressure people feel in a family. They tend to deal with one another again; often they deal with one another for the rest of their lives. Their reputation and social status is on the line, and if they break their agreements they know they have to face hostility from someone with whom they are in close personal contact. This, more than the law, keeps them honest. This is how primitive societies work.

The advantage is clear—people know one another and do not need complicated laws or rules or regulations to force them to keep their agreements; there is an intimacy and predictability in this economic order. The downside is that you can only trade for the goods and services that can be produced within the small society in which you live. Goods and services produced at far distances or goods and services produced by villages with technological capacities that your village lacks are not available to you. The only wealth you have access to in a primitive society is the wealth that can be created by that primitive society. And, so, primitive societies never reached high levels of economic development. This all changed, according to Friedrich Hayek in his book *The Fatal Conceit*, when the Western world began what he called "an extended order," or "an extended order of civilization."

In Hayek's conception of the extended order, economic activity moved from the village level to the regional, national, or even international level, through a set of rules and laws that enabled people to trade goods and services with people outside their little village and perhaps outside their own country. This development in civilization extends the order of civilization over vastly greater distances. It allows people to trade with others whom they have not met, nor ever will.

The extended order allows people to trade goods and services not only over long distances but over numerous steps in the economic production process. In other words, somebody in China can produce a component that he sells to somebody in Australia, who buys that component along with other components from someone in Malaysia and Singapore and Germany and South Africa, combining them into a machine or a toy or an automobile that they then sell to an auto-distribution company in Europe, which then markets the automobile to someone in Pittsburgh, Pennsylvania.

The transactions that occur before I and my family buy a car literally number in the thousands and no one person in this chain knows more than a few people out of the thousands throughout the chain. So what holds it together? What holds it together is contract law, a complex and intricate system of rules that cause people to keep agreements with people with whom they have never dealt before, and with whom they may never deal again. It has become a system that is so dependable that it doesn't require a handshake. Nobody looks somebody else in the eye. This system of laws, courts, financing, and banking makes it possible for commodities to go from someplace in the world to China and Malaysia and Singapore through numerous transactions involving many different currencies. So, maybe it starts in a South African rand and then becomes a Malaysian ringgit, and then a Chinese yuan, and then an Australian dollar, before it's eventually translated into an American dollar. No one person understands the whole system. No one authority enforces a whole system, but a system of common law arises over time that is so reliable that trillions of dollars can travel around the world: trillions of dollars in currency and goods and services can travel around the world every day based on nothing more than the authority of contracts. This causes our economic order to be extended. We combine efforts from people all around the world, which means I can get something here in America that nobody in America knows how to make. Goods and services come from all around the world, which lowers the price of the clothing you buy at Walmart because of the intense competition between all of these economic actors in a world of 7 billion people.

And so we've had a standard of living that is astronomically advanced compared to just a few hundred years ago and incomparably higher than in a primitive village. The disadvantage is that as politicians, thought leaders, economic actors, and popular cultures gradually begin to develop an attitude toward contracts in which their sanctity is increasingly called into question, the extended order begins to disintegrate. In other words, as the contracts that we make with people we don't know take second place to the desires, needs, or convenience of the moment, the economic order teeters toward at least partial collapse.

For example, let's look at the current economic crisis in the world's mortgage markets, which illustrates these principles very well. There was a time when loans were made before a small group of people. Remember the movie *It's a Wonderful Life*? The proprietor of the Bailey Building and Loan, George Bailey, takes in deposits from citizens of his town, Bedford Falls, and then uses those deposits to issue home mortgages to other citizens of Bedford Falls. In one particularly interesting scene, there is a run on the bank fomented by a lack of confidence in the soundness of the institution. At one particular moment in the crisis George Bailey asks one particular man not to withdraw all of his money from the bank. The man insists on taking it out immediately. And in a stirring description of fractional reserve banking, he explains that the man's money isn't there. He tells him that his money is in the homes of the other people in the crowd, and he points them out by name, assuring him that his neighbors are "good for it." That's a traditional system of financing home purchases.

Over time, our political class in Washington decided that the old system was not sufficiently generous in offering credit to people who want to buy homes. The new system would induce them to make more loans to more applicants, to put more people into homes. And so the government set up an agency that purchases home loans from the Bailey Buildings and Loans of the world. Eventually these government entities were privatized and sent out into the marketplace, where they began to package these mortgages into groups of one thousand and sell them out into the world. Now the depositor, the person lending the money, could be in Singapore as well as in Bedford Falls, and so the familial, tribal, and social bonds no longer apply. The only thing that compels the borrower to repay the lender is the sanctity of the contract as guaranteed by the common law and the Constitution. What we've found in our current time of crisis and in times of leftward political drift is that these rules of contract are seen as archaic, arbitrary, and breakable at will. And so we have seen discussions, largely in the Democratic Party, of ideas as radical as taking away the rights of the lender to foreclose on the property if the borrower no longer makes good-faith efforts to pay his mortgage. We've seen efforts to give judges the authority to unilaterally lower the interest rates on the loan and thereby diminish the amount due to the lender. What we've seen is the erosion of the idea of the sanctity of a contract. In a situation where there is a political drift to the left, increasingly we see the acid of leftism applied to the links in the chain that connect one part of the globe to another. The potency of that acid and the vulnerability of the chain limit the degree to which this extended order—about which Hayek wrote was the basis of modern civilization—can extend. To the degree that we are no longer willing to enforce the abstract principle of the sanctity of contracts to the benefit of people who we do not personally know, but instead favor people who are our neighbors or members of the same race, religion, or nation-state because of our tribal bond, and to allow them to break their commitments to those who lie outside of our little village, to that degree our system of financial order must disintegrate. This must mean a contraction of the amount of wealth around the world. The long process of going from small village, to city, to city-state, to nation, to global marketplace, which has taken us from bare subsistence to the highest standard of living in human history, is beginning to be thrown into reverse.

This is what Ludwig von Mises, Hayek's mentor, described as economic disintegration. If we pass laws that say that everyone is permitted to stay in their homes no matter what, it

creates the appearance of stability because on the surface everyone gets to stay in their home. But in fact it creates tremendous
instability, because in reality everyone is forced out of their
contracts. And if everyone is forced out of their contracts, then
there can be no more lending, and with no more lending there
can be no more new homes. That, of course, is what happens
if we drive this new ideology to its logical conclusion. These
problems are solvable, but they require changes in the way we
invest and launch businesses, and changes in the way we plan
our careers to account for the leftward and populist drift that
has already begun in our political and economic order.

The move toward affinity business relationships poses new
dangers for investors, which are represented most clearly in the
Bernie Madoff scandal, which came to light in the winter of
2008.

Bernie Madoff perpetrated the largest Ponzi scheme in U.S.
history. This we already know. Everyone on TV has made the
Ponzi observation in terms of the mechanics of the scam, but
I'm more interested in a more direct historical parallel. Both
scandals depended on ethnic and religious tribalization as an
environment favorable to deception. Ponzi was able to do what
he did because he used religious and ethnic affinity. He didn't
scam the world in general; he scammed the Italian-American
community. There was a strong element of tribalism and identity politics in what he did. He dealt with Italian-owned banks,
with the Italian mob, and with Italian cultural institutions. He
played up his Italian heritage. He was considered to be a hero
by many in the Italian-American community.

My point is that affinity networks, religious and cultural, are
particularly vulnerable to this kind of manipulation. I suspect
that this may be especially true if they've lost their religious
moorings. Think about what used to unite Jews as Jews—the

Torah. "Jewish" used to mean Torah-observant. It didn't mean a certain accent, or inclusion in certain country clubs, or food choices. It meant the people chosen by God to be the bearer of the Law.

In order to steal so much money from the Jewish community, Madoff would have had to walk down many hallways and into many rooms in which the Ten Commandments were posted. He would have walked through synagogues and Jewish Foundation offices and Yeshiva University conference rooms. Hundreds of times he would have walked past a plaque that read *lo tegnav*—Thou Shalt Not Steal. But it didn't penetrate Madoff's heart. He did not heed the prophet's instruction to write the Law of God in his heart.

And what of the people who entrusted their assets, and more disturbingly, the assets of charities with which they were charged to him? Why were they so easily manipulated?

People who are part of affinity groups tend to suspend their critical judgment when approached through the language and mores of the tribe. The presidential candidate Mike Huckabee bragged to a group of pastors that he "spoke the mother tongue of Zion," meaning that, unlike John McCain or Mitt Romney, he spoke evangelical-ese fluently. What is this if not a signal to his coreligionists to drop their shields and offer their trust without skepticism? Commentators rightly identified this as a form of "Christian identity politics."

Years ago, a scandal rocked the Christian world in the form of the New Era Foundation. This scam was also mechanically identical to a Ponzi scheme. It also was philanthropically connected. New Era likewise tapped into an affinity group. The crooks at New Era "spoke the mother tongue of Zion," and they did it with as much facility as they violated the commandments housed on Mount Zion.

The thing that makes the Madoff scam so much bigger than New Era is that it is, well, so much bigger. There's no way any smooth-talking preacher could talk $50 billion out of his brethren—they're not rich enough. The Manhattan–Palm Beach Jewish community is a different story. There are huge financial resources there. But is there still huge financial wisdom there? Would this scam have been viable two generations ago? Would first-generation Jewish immigrants, who had fought their way up through extremely adverse economic circumstances, have been so easily separated from their money?

I doubt it.

But a few generations later, many such families moved from hardscrabble, full-body-contact entrepreneurship to the Ivy League, trust funds, and credentialed professions. Perhaps there is more money there than there is judgment. Grandpa Saul worked impossible hours and made his own cash deposits in rough neighborhoods. Grandson Aaron is a cardiologist and on the board of the hospital. Saul would have sent Madoff out the door with a none-too-subtle kick in the keister. Aaron, on the other hand, wants to get invited to the right parties.

Madoff's clients depended on inherited social networks for their sense of safety. Madoff himself depended on inherited social networks for his hunting grounds.

LET'S TAKE A few permanent lessons from this painful experience:

Lesson 1: You don't have to believe in the hereafter to know what some people are here after. When someone approaches me about business and they throw around common religious buzzwords, I run away.

Lesson 2: "Pride goeth before a fall," said Solomon, son of David, King of Israel. For every major character defect deduct at least ten points from an investor's IQ, but for pride, deduct thirty. Investors who believe that they or their social set are too smart to be swindled are in fact too foolish to keep their wealth.

Lesson 3: "I'd rather be governed by a competent Turk than by an incompetent Christian."—Martin Luther. Religious affinity is no guarantee of effective money management. Don't go with the guy who sounds like you, go with the guy who makes sense to you. When they read his reports, no one had any idea what Madoff was talking about. That should have been warning enough.

I've painted a picture of a financial world that may depend more on relationships that on contracts. A world more tribalized than recent history is what I expect. It is what you should be prepared for. This means extra care in the particular areas of vulnerability that emerge in affinity networks. Ponzi schemes and other trust-based scams should be at the top of your list. A wise investor should look for independent verification of character and competence outside of the affinity group. He should place genuine evidence of character, or true piety, ahead of status-maximizing religious affirmations or high-profile acts of ostentatious humanitarianism. He is willing to seek business outside of his particular ethnic or religious affinity network when he has reason to believe that there is a more reliable and ethical prospect elsewhere. By doing this, he puts himself in the middle of a number of networks with the ability to function in whichever one fits the given transaction most closely. Use the new affinity economy wisely, but don't abuse it. Don't be abused by it.

# CHAPTER FIVE

# Principles for Surfing the Socialism

lassical economics is the discipline, starting with Adam Smith and proceeding through J. B. Say and down through Ludwig von Mises, Friedrich Hayek, and Arthur Laffer, that studies the true patterns of economics. The great political philosophers—William Shakespeare, Francis Bacon, John Locke, Thomas Jefferson, James Madison, Alexis de Tocqueville (and their modern followers)—study the true patterns of politics, including the ways in which it is likely to intervene in the markets. These two models, classical economics and classical modern political theory, are more effective than anything we have seen so far in helping us to understand the world of money and politics and to prosper in both. There is almost nothing in this book that does not come from my three-decade study of these great minds.

Socialism is chaos, but it is predictable chaos. Like that of tsunamis, hurricanes, or earthquakes, socialism's destruction is patterned. And what is patterned can be anticipated, and what is anticipated can often be profited from. Price ceilings cause shortages; price floors cause gluts. Supply disruptions cause price hikes. Supply subsidies cause price troughs. These shortages, gluts, price increases and decreases ripple out through the markets for alternate goods through substitution effects. The people clamor for relief and the central planners react in predictable ways. They have few choices between alternative courses, whether they know it or not. They can give up power and face shame and humiliation, or they can shift the blame to someone else. They can tell the hungry urban populace that the increase in the price of bread is a matter of greedy middlemen in the grocery stores. They can impose price controls to punish the vendors. When the bread disappears from the shelves, the central planners can blame hoarders in the agribusiness sector and expropriate their inventory. When investors refuse to lend money to farmers the following year, the planners can declare that the market has failed, and nationalize the larger farms.

This scenario is unlikely in America; farmers are a favored political interest group at the moment. It has played out dozens of times in the past century, however. But substitute "banker" for "farmer," "Wall Street" for "agriculture," and "credit" for "bread" and the pattern of mandate, price spike, price control, shortage, and nationalization does not seem in the least bit far-fetched.

This kind of government control always produces winners and losers. The winners are politically powerful; the losers are not. Knowing in advance who the winners and losers are enables you to avoid being one of the latter.

## Move Taxes to Center Stage

The higher your taxes are, the more they matter. That's why, in order to become the kind of investor who is suited to the current anti-investor environment, you have to change your old way of thinking. In times of comparatively low tax rates, investors concentrate almost exclusively on eking out a few more points of return on their investments. The problem with that view now is that focusing attention on a few more percentage points' gain, in an environment where percentage points gained are hard to come by, and not on percentage points saved in taxes is a formula for wealth destruction.

We don't know how high taxes are going to go. As of this writing, the Obama administration has already broken its promise that it would only raise taxes on families making $250,000 or more. The president has proposed raising people at the 33 percent rate to a 35 percent rate, and cutting back on their allowable tax deductions for such items as charitable contributions, mortgage interest, and state and local taxes paid. That affects people starting at $165,000 per year.

In addition, the new health care regime threatens a system of "penalties" for businesses that do not offer a certain minimum level of health care benefits (to be determined by the government) to its employees. This is a tax. Fees imposed on tanning salons, medical device manufacturers, and high-value health insurance plans are taxes. Greater restrictions on the use of health savings account (HSA) money, such as disallowing vitamin supplements, is a tax. And of course, doubling the excise tax for withdrawals from HSAs is a tax, too.

And in an environment where health care costs are socialized, can sugar and fat taxes be far behind? The principal argument against taxes on fats and sugar was based on personal liberty. But that argument loses appeal if we're all paying for each other's stents. So in the blizzard of nanny-state nuisance taxes that is blowing our way, there is almost certainly a tax on literal Blizzards, and many of Dairy Queen's other frosty delights.

Furthermore, although Obama promised not to raise corporate tax rates, he did pledge to close "loopholes" for corporations in the tax code. If the government keeps your statutory tax rate the same, and decreases your deductions, then your taxes are going up. Your actual taxes paid as a percentage of your profit (known to us bean counters as "effective tax rate") go up.

In addition, it is a near certainty that the administration will increase payroll taxes on top earners. You see, under the current system, since wealthy earners face a cap in their Social Security benefits, they are protected by a cap on their taxes paid. Since, at its inception, Social Security was promoted as an insurance program, and not a welfare program, it was deemed necessary that there be some relationship between what you pay into the system and what you take out of it. Billionaires don't get million-dollar Social Security checks, so they shouldn't be forced to pay million-dollar premiums.

Obama's proposal would change all of that. Social Security would leave off all pretense of being an insurance or pension plan into which you make contributions that will be returned to you later. It will become just another transfer program, plain and simple. This will be a real killer for higher-income earners.

Some of this is already scheduled to begin with the phase-in of the health care plan, which imposes a nearly 4 percent tax on affluent investors.

Finally, investment taxes themselves have already increased dramatically.

As the super-economist Arthur Laffer has pointed out, these tax policies cause huge, unsustainable budget holes. The alleged Obama tax cuts really amount to transfer payments from the wealthy and the upper middle class to everyone else. These transfer payments amount to nearly a total loss to the federal budget. At the lower income levels, people do not respond very dynamically to tax cuts, because the tax burdens are so low to begin with. People don't change their economic behavior much in response to such incentives as moving their take-home pay from 93 percent of earnings up to, say, 95 percent of earnings. On the other hand, people do modify their behavior if you allow them to take home 70 percent of what they make as opposed to 50 percent of it.

This effect is magnified by the fact that wealthy people, especially business owners, have more control over their earnings than do wage earners. The latter generally don't have any discretion in their earnings, except the occasional decision whether to accept overtime hours. I expect that overtime hours may be relatively scarce during this period anyway. So, if you send a government check to a lower-middle-class wage employee, he generally saves it. If you convince him that the checks will keep coming for a long, long time, he'll generally spend it. What he probably will not do is change his working habits so as to maximize his income in reaction to the lower effective tax rate, especially since he runs the risk of pushing it high enough that the government checks will shrink or disappear. You just don't get revenue increases this way.

On the other hand, entrepreneurs and professional investors have enormous leeway when it comes to control over their financial lives. They can sell a security at a time of minimum taxes to harvest the gain at the lowest possible cost. They can hold those assets during periods of high taxes, hoping to hold out till the rates come down again. They can choose to invest their money or their efforts in tax-favored or tax-excluded enterprises. They can sell securities, the value of which is depressed and likely to stay that way, during times of high rates so as to harvest the losses to maximum benefit. They are in control. They modify their behavior to suit the times. They have professional tax advisors who keep them abreast of changes in the code in advance of their decisions. If they are top earners they don't worry about whether they're going to make too much money, which will propel them into a higher bracket, because they're already in the highest bracket. They don't worry that earning more money will cost them a government check, because they're not the ones who get the government checks.

Raise tax rates on these people, and revenues plunge. They know how to hide.

So transfer payments to the bottom and higher taxes to the top both yield the same result: lower tax revenues. And since Obama has promised a rather dizzying array of new public spending initiatives, and since both domestic politics and skeptical Chinese bond buyers limit the amount that he can borrow, tax hikes even more aggressive than those initially proposed are quite likely.

For all of these reasons, tax planning is now your most important investment strategy.

LET'S START WITH the easy ideas:

Diligence matters. I'm not going to give you what is so easily available in any of the dozen or so "tax guides" that are published every year and contain the basics of tax planning. They tell you all about home office deductions and about various pension planning tools, such as 401(k), IRA, SEPP, Keogh, and Roth IRA accounts. They'll give you long lists (whole books full of them) with ideas for deductions you might have missed, such as special clothing and work-related educational expenses. They'll tell you how to document charitable contributions and urge you to make donations of clothing and other qualified items to Goodwill and other charitable institutions and to save the receipts. You don't need me for that. What you need from me is the admonition that all of that just became much more important. Don't neglect it. If you've been on the bubble before about using someone outside versus preparing your own tax returns, it's probably time to use an outside preparer. The code is complex and, since the Obama playbook includes using the code for social engineering, it is about to get much more complex. The accountant will pay for himself.

Speaking of social engineering through the tax code: don't fall for it. It's not free money. If it makes good sense for you to weatherproof your home, then do it. But don't collect the flood of information about how to cash in on the Obama tax credit carrot-and-stick program and start to structure your life accordingly. You will change in ways that are not in the long-term interest of you and your family. Chasing government carrots tends to change people. They lose their business edge and substitute it with an appetite to get their due. There are plenty of fat books out there that give you advice on how to get government money. Ignore them. Don't invest your future in socialism. It is a passing fad that has been rejected by every sane nation that has ever tried it. Don't invest yourself in its continuation. Don't mold your mind in that direction. Do what makes good financial sense for you and yours for the long run, and by all means use any tax advantage you can once you've made your decision. But keep your priorities in line. It's easy for people to set their goal as getting government tax credits and then structure their financial life to serve that goal. Set out your financial strategy first. If your tax advisor can use some of those decisions to get a refund check for you, that's fine. Otherwise, you will have built your financial life in a quest for a tax reward that will either disappear when America comes back to her senses, as she always has in the past, or if she does not come back to her senses, you will find the government micromanaging your decisions more and more closely, requiring you to jump through ever smaller and more intricate hoops.

Eventually you'll find yourself owning nothing but unionized wind farms built in formerly blighted urban neighborhoods surrounded by snail-darter-filled swamps that you are not allowed to drain, and all of it wheelchair accessible. And the tax credits will be phased out for fat cats like you anyway. When faced with a choice between carrots and sticks, choose the third option. Don't be the donkey.

So IF YOU don't focus on the current wave of small-bore social engineering tax credits, what should you focus on? You should focus on tax principles that have existed for long periods of time and are deeply ingrained in our legal, financial, and political culture. Retirement planning is one of them. Though it is not perfectly unassailable, it has been amazingly durable over several generations.

There are basically two kinds of retirement plans: defined benefit plans and defined contribution plans. They are generally known as DBs and DCs, respectively. DBs are your father's pension plan; he worked for a certain number of years at the plant, and as a reward for his decades of service to the same company he gets a certain monthly retirement check, which is determined by a formula based on his years of service and his income during those years of service. DCs are *your* pension plan. You put a certain amount away every year, and within certain parameters you decide how it is to be invested. Your retirement benefit is not determined in advance, but varies according to how well your investments did. The Left loves the former and hates the latter. This can be used to your advantage.

You are not used to thinking of DBs as an option. They have been steadily losing market share to more up-to-date DC plans. They are about to become more popular. I'm not saying that you should give up your 401(k). In fact, I think that if you don't have one, or an IRA or a Roth, you should set one up immediately. Get one started while you still can. Plans like this are almost always "grandfathered in"—that is, even during times of hostility to setting up new market-based DC plans, when it will become harder to start one, the already existing ones will be permitted to continue. At least, that's been the pattern in the past. I don't want you to swap your DC for a DB; I want you to add a DB on top. The regulations are favorable to that right now and moving ever more favorably as I write. The Left doesn't like it when people's retirements are tied up in the market. They don't want you to be an owner. They don't want you to be dependent on what they see as the cruel and irrational vicissitudes of the market. They don't want you to vote the way shareholders vote. They want all pension plans, public and private, to look and feel like Social Security. They are willing to grant strong tax incentives to make this happen. If you are clever, you can do what you already want to do anyway, which is to accumulate capital for you and your family, and to do it with tremendous tax advantages. Small businesses are in a particularly good position to do this. They won't really intend to turn mom-and-pop shops into providers of DB pension plans, but they won't be able to stop it. In order to get the big boys to move back to traditional pension plans, they will have to offer rewards that they dare not deny to the little guys. Remember, small business (or as Obama sometimes puts it—the smallest businesses) are a politically protected class. To attack them is to admit that the Left's alleged populism is a ruse.

Hybrid DB-DC plans are about to become a very powerful way to shield assets in an anti-asset environment. Offering DC plans to all will be part of the formula, but the younger workers will be able to take the most advantage of it. The DB formulas will be very favorable to older employees, which usually means the owner and (if she works for the business) the wife. Since the government wants these plans to exist and to be well funded, they give enormous latitude to these senior employees to take large tax deductions as they get closer and closer to retirement. The only significant limits in the past have been something called "anti-discrimination" rules, which are designed to stop the employers from loading up their own pension plans and discriminating against their younger workers. The irony of this is that the smaller the workforce, the less of an issue the anti-discrimination issues are. In other words, if the business is run by a husband and wife and has a few, usually younger, employees, the anti-discrimination rules are hardly a problem at all. They have enormous discretion to sock money away tax-free. The central planners have created yet another (there are others) incentive to keep employment low, to use technology rather than people, and to use subcontractors rather than employees.

All of this is detailed and technical stuff. Your accountant probably can't do it. You'll need an actuary to design these plans. But if you are a business owner with a big tax bill and a desire to shield capital from the tax man, you should definitely get your accountant and an actuary in the same room (or at least on the same conference call) and get them to analyze a hybrid DB-DC plan.

. . . .

TAXES ALSO HAVE a major immediate impact on investment decisions. There is a continuum of what the industry calls "tax efficiency." Some investments receive very favorable tax treatment; some receive very unfavorable tax treatment. For example, municipal bonds are, as a general rule, a source of tax-free income. But there are exceptions to this rule. For one, municipal bonds that are deemed to be "private activity bonds"—that is, bonds whose proceeds are used to build facilities that primarily benefit private entities—may trigger an Alternative Minimum Tax liability. So, stadium or airport bonds are not as tax-efficient as other municipal bonds. Also, the way you as an investor treat your bonds can make them more or less tax-efficient to you. Interest from municipal bonds is tax-free, but if you sell your bonds at a gain, then the capital gain is taxable. This is all very complex. So don't rush out and load up on munis without consulting a tax or financial advisor.

Tax shelters, at least at one point in their life cycle, are extremely efficient. Now they are nearly extinct. At one point limited liability partnerships that owned real estate were extremely popular, especially in the 1970s. The real estate would generate positive cash flow for the investors, but depreciation rules would amazingly produce noncash tax losses that would flow through to the same investors. You made money, but got to report theoretical losses. Too good to be true, right? So Congress changed the rules, and the poor schnooks who bought these were left with cash losses and taxable gains. This is a highly risky tax-minimization strategy. I would not recommend it. I was a professional tax advisor in the late 1980s, when these tax shelters were eliminated. Perhaps the trauma of calculating my clients' financial losses and tax liabilities was enough to create a permanent stimulus-and-response bond between tax gimmicks and pain. Perhaps my S and R bond can help you to avoid some of your own trauma.

Payroll income is very tax-inefficient. You have to pay income taxes on it (top rate about to move to 40 percent) and you have to pay payroll taxes on top of that (top rate going to who knows where). You are generally not permitted many deductions from it, either, like business expenses. Business income, generally known as "schedule C income" because it is calculated on Schedule C of Form 1040, is a little better than payroll. You can deduct some business expenses, but still pay the relatively high personal income tax rate on it. Ordinary income brought in through a sole proprietorship is more tax-efficient than the type that comes through an incorporated entity when it comes to some payroll taxes. Capital gains are more efficient than ordinary income, especially when they are long-term gains. If certain conditions are met, long-term capital gains on certain start-up companies will be very tax-efficient. ETFs (exchange-traded funds) are generally more tax efficient than mutual funds because they give the investor control over when to trigger capital gains and losses. This is important, because the ability to determine when to "harvest" losses enables you to use those losses to offset gains incurred during that same year, cutting your tax bill.

As a general rule, the higher your tax rate, the more emphasis you should place on the tax efficiency of your investments. Ironically, our current wave of left-wing political populism gives great advantages to business owners (who have a great deal of flexibility in structuring their financial lives in tax-efficient ways) and professional investors, and gives comparative disadvantages to wage and salary workers, at least to those whose income is high enough to actually pay income taxes.

Family-owned businesses have tremendous potential for tax efficiency. Children can work for the family business and be compensated at levels that fall below the *de minimus* levels for taxable income for income and payroll taxes. This shifts family income from the higher tax brackets for Mom and Pop to the lower (or even nonexistent) tax rates of the children. For minor children, some of that pay can be placed into custodial accounts and used for the children's household expenses.

It is even possible to pay the (major or minor) children in stock rather than cash, costing the business no money at all (though it dilutes the parents' equity in the company), shifting the income from the higher taxable rates of the parents to the lower taxable rates of the children. Instead of waiting until death or retirement and transferring ownership of the business to the next generation, often at very high inheritance tax rates, you transfer the assets year by year and get a tax deduction for doing so. I think there are very strong non-tax-related reasons for doing this. I've seen what sudden transfers of wealth from one generation to another can do to the recipients and the results are frequently heartbreaking. There are good reasons to consider gradualism when it comes to intergenerational wealth preservation.

I have wandered somewhat away from pure financial analysis into a major lifestyle question. The Bowyers have taken this approach to wealth succession and have been very happy with the results.

I EXPECT TO see a major shift away from the profit-seeking sector of the economy to the nonprofit sector. Given Barack and Michelle Obama's many statements deriding the former and praising the latter, it is probable that this shift is consciously intended. As mentioned earlier, when Obama worked briefly for a Wall Street firm, according to his memoirs he "felt like a spy behind enemy lines." Michelle Obama bragged to a group of social workers that she and her husband had not gone for the cash, but had worked in the service and nonprofit sectors giving back to the community. As a matter of fact, Michelle herself worked for the public relations department of a large hospital. Shortly after Barack became a state senator, her pay was doubled from $175,000 to $350,000 per year. Apparently "giving back" is even more fulfilling than most people realize.

The Left demonizes the world of profit and idolizes the world of philanthropy. Expect to see policies that penalize the former and reward the latter. Talent will shift from the besieged sectors to the benighted ones. This has innumerable investment, career, and entrepreneurial implications. Expect to see more ease in donating assets that have increased in value to charitable causes. Expect to see donor development for large charitable organizations become a more appealing career track than it has been in the past. Expect to see businesses that in the past would probably have been organized as profit-seeking businesses appear in a nonprofit form. Educational institutions can be for-profit or nonprofit. So can publishing enterprises. If you are about to start a small business, stop for a moment and talk to your accountant and see whether your business would qualify under section 501(c)3 as a tax-exempt charitable institution. Would that designation be advantageous to you? Want to tutor kids in math, or teach adults computer skills? Want to publish books or newsletters? Want to broadcast radio or TV shows? How about helping businesses band together and purchase health insurance in a co-op? In an age in which our leaders hate profit and love charities, you may want to wrap your qualified business plan in the form of the latter rather than the former. Nonprofits can generate large surpluses of revenues over expenses, whether they technically call them profits or not.

## Time to Get Small

It may sound counterintuitive, but anti-wealth political climates present excellent times to start a small business.

To begin with, entrepreneurship carries many tax planning advantages: If you were paid as a 1099 contractor, you can deduct many expenses on your Schedule C that you would not be allowed to deduct if you were a traditional employee of a corporation. Educational materials, transportation, and pretty much anything pertaining to your business can be taken as a deduction in calculating your profit from your small business. If you incorporate, you can open additional tax-sheltered IRAs, as well as compensate employees and family in stock, which can in turn be deducted. For family businesses there are some truly astounding tax benefits to be had in transferring ownership to the next generation. Compensating family members in stock in your company solves the age-old problem of the "trust fund" kid who grows up without business experience or any sense of economic scarcity, until suddenly one day the entire family fortune is dropped into his or her lap without the child's having had any significant role in the creation of that wealth. Many a wealthy leftist emerges on that day, assuaging the guilt for receiving wealth for which he did not labor by giving some of it to socialist causes. Wealth creation is the opposite of sausage making; it is generally appreciated more by those who see it being made. Payroll tax can be reduced by compensating owners and shareholders as partnership income (K-1).

For the moment let's focus on the business side of small business.

Antigrowth political leaders tend to couch their central planning ideology in terms of populism. If a powerful man, with many very wealthy friends, asks you for more power, he's likely to do it by playing up his credibility as a regular guy. He'll drop the letter *g* from his participles: no more working men, only workin' men. No more playing by the rules, only playin' by the rules. I think this is supposed to sound rural or something (oops, somethin'), but the tone is definitely diminutive. It says, "I'm not a big man; I'm just like you."

The populist routine is bolstered with attacks on large companies. The word "big" moves from neutral status to an automatic term of abuse. No politician labels an industry "big" if he plans to lessen its tax or regulatory burden. You never hear, except from the right, about "big solar" or "big ethanol," although that latter industry has grown quite large indeed. "Big Tobacco, Oil, Pharma, Insurance" . . . if you hear a politician, who is in a position to enact policy, use the word "big" in reference to a sector, then it is time to reduce the size of your portfolio in that sector.

Even the violent socialist movements of the twentieth century focused their attention on what Lenin called "the commanding heights" of the economy: mining, electricity, and banking. Those political targets are easier to justify. On the other hand, it is pretty difficult to position oneself as on the side of the little guy if one goes around nationalizing family farms, restaurants, and corner stores.

In the political tug-of-war, small business gets a pass from people who generally don't like any business, because an attack on small business would remove the populist mask. I knew Hillary Clinton's health care plan was doomed the day she told a Republican congressman that "I can't be held responsible for every little undercapitalized business out there." In other words, if they can't afford to pay my extra health care tax, they don't deserve to be in business in the first place.

Team Obama has studied the Clinton health care debacle the way a team that lost the Super Bowl studies the painful footage of the game, looking for the mistakes and fixing them. Even during the campaign, Senator Obama talked about small business exemptions for fines imposed on firms that do not pay health insurance benefits. In an interesting switch, however, he referred to "the smallest businesses," not, per usual, to "small businesses." When pressed for more details, one of his advisors mentioned businesses with ten or fewer employees. Why ten, a suspiciously round number? Ten is a political number, not an economic one. There's nothing economically magical about ten as opposed to nine or eleven employees, but the threshold does seem to define what American voters would see as the smallest, as opposed to just small, businesses. Eventually Team Obama settled on fifty employees as the cutoff point between mandated and non-mandated companies.

Of course, they'd like to go after all the businesses no matter how small. Hillary tried to. So did the unions when they pushed hard for ergonomic standards for home-based businesses. They are fully aware of the threat that the small business revolution represents to big labor (yes, by "big" I mean "bad"). But they failed. There is enough of a sense of freedom left in the American psyche, bruised and battered by demagogues and business-bashing pop culture as it is, that rebels against the idea of guys with clipboards standing in our home offices without our consent.

This means that there is currently a shift of economic activity from large businesses to small ones. This will hurt our standard of living. Large businesses can be almost incredibly productive. Economies of scale, the effect that allows some products to be produced much more cheaply in very large quantities, is one of the most powerful engines of economic growth ever seen. In fact, the consumer revolution could not have occurred without it. Some things can be done very cost-effectively on a small scale, such as haircuts, psychiatry, lawn mowing, and catering. But there are no mom-and-pop electricity companies of any real significance. Many things simply cannot be done without enormous pools of capital. Utilities, railroads, and commercial airlines are by their very nature large enterprises.

Yes, there are some manufacturing processes that can be done on a small scale, but generally not for the masses. I have a friend who builds wooden canoes by hand. I have a family member who builds custom cabinets. But these products are quite expensive, and only wealthy people can afford them. When I want a canoe, I go to the sporting goods store and buy a mass-produced one. If I want a cabinet, it's Walmart or maybe Costco, which are able to buy in huge bulk from companies that buy their raw materials in even larger bulk and amortize their design and marketing costs over an astounding number of units created.

Don't romanticize small business. If tough regulation of big companies pushes economic activity down to the small ones, then consumers will be hurt. I recommend that you begin to think in terms of small business as a personal wealth-building strategy, a kind of city of refuge from the big (yes, as in bad) state.

What kind of small business should you start? Well, the kind you're good at. Immersing yourself in a brand-new field makes little economic sense if you already have a good foundation in some other field. I'm going to tell you where I think the opportunities lie now, but that doesn't mean I recommend that you go into tax planning if you're no good at math and your wife (or H&R Block) does your returns every year.

The broad principle is this: Anti-wealth political climates harm certain groups of people more than others. Protecting the harmed groups is good business during such times.

## Investing in a Jobless Recovery

Welfare states suffer from long-term economic stagnation. To guard against that gnawing fear of poverty and unemployment, the rulers of such societies turn toward policies that create a high degree of job security. It becomes nearly impossible to fire an incompetent, or even to cut his pay. Unions become the real managers of major corporations and push for ever more extensive benefits and vacation packages. Businesses, finding themselves unable to fire someone once they've been hired, stop hiring altogether. Paradoxically, social welfare states tend to have higher than normal levels of unemployment. In America we hire easily, because we can fire at will. If the employee doesn't work well, we have the flexibility to undo the mistake quickly and easily. But in countries where employment agreements are presumed to be as permanent as marriages (or more than), they are entered into with great caution.

This employment pattern has tremendous implications for U.S. investors and entrepreneurs who are looking for ways to survive under Obama. It means that we should assume much less labor flexibility than we are used to seeing. This means that unemployment will drop much more slowly as the economy recovers from the recession than it dropped when we left prior ones. Employers have been much less quick to staff up in a world where they are going to be unable to quickly downsize.

Some employers, especially those under direct or indirect control of the government, will hire in response to political pressure. Some employers will staff up because they simply will not have fully realized what the new rules are. Smart entrepreneurs will not do much hiring at all. They will use their current workforce to do more work. They will hold on to their best people during the dip, and then when the dip is over they will offer them overtime, or higher salaries to do more work. They will leverage technology more, showering their high-productivity employees with laptops, BlackBerrys, voice-recognition software, video conferencing, flextime, and anything else the top people need in order to do the work of two or three. When new people are absolutely needed, they will be brought on as subcontractors or on loan from temp agencies. Temp agencies and outsourcing shops are becoming important tools for large companies looking for labor market flexibility at a time when the rules are against flexibility. Both types of business are good targets for investment or entrepreneurial start-up ideas, especially for businesses that do not have high levels of unionization and therefore have not already signed away their rights to outsource.

Stupid managers learn through mistakes. They find themselves with large, low-pay workforces, sitting ducks for card check unionization drives. Even if card check per se does not pass (and I think it will not), some scaled-down version will find its way through. President Obama owes his primary victory to the Service Employees International Union (SEIU) and they want to unionize large retailers (like Walmart) and the nursing home industry. They'll get a lot of what they want.

The businesses in the best position are those with small, highly skilled, highly compensated, highly productive workforces. Own those.

## The Catacomb Economy

We have a historical precedent to look to as we search for strategies that enable us to surf the socialism—America in the 1970s. LBJ created huge bureaucracies with massive cost centers. Nixon did nothing to roll back the spending, delinked the dollar from any real store of value, and then imposed wage and price controls to forbid the inflation he had created. Carter upped the ante by centralizing control of the petroleum market in the state. Was it full-bore socialism? No, but it was close enough to saddle America with a decade of inflationary stagnation, a noxious cocktail that previously had been considered impossible to create.

But all was not stagnant. Beneath the surface, the next generation of businesses was germinating. My good friend Rich Karlgaard, the publisher of *Forbes*, has the list:

**Southwest Airlines**—Conceived over drinks by Herb Kelleher and Rollin King in 1966, Air Southwest was mired in legal difficulties until 1970. In 1971 the company changed its name to Southwest Airlines and made its first flight in June of that year.

**FedEx**—Founded in Little Rock, Arkansas, by Fred Smith in 1971, Federal Express made a smart move in 1973, just as jet fuel prices were spiraling out of control. Smith moved his company to Memphis, Tennessee, and hatched the super-hub concept that would give his company a huge efficiency advantage.

**Microsoft**—Bill Gates dropped out of Harvard and talked his friend Paul Allen into joining him in Albuquerque, New Mexico, to start Micro-Soft. The company's first product was an adaptation of the Basic programming language used in the Altair 8800, a kit computer. . . .

**Apple**—Steve Jobs and Steve Wozniak formed Apple Computer in 1976 to sell the Apple I personal computer kit. Each was hand-built by Woz. A year later the company launched the Apple II, considered by many to be the first personal computer useful for business tasks. . . .

**Oracle**—In 1977, Larry Ellison, Bob Miner, and Ed Oates founded Software Development Laboratories around a new IBM . . . technology called relational databases. The company's first product was called the Oracle database and outperformed IBM. In 1982, the company was renamed Oracle Systems.

—RICH KARLGAARD, "DIGITAL RULES: A NEW WAVE OF
ENTREPRENEURS?" *Forbes*, NOVEMBER 10, 2008

Look closely at that list. Do you see how many of these companies are using new models or new technologies to solve problems created by government central planning? Both FedEx and Southwest were partly designed to deal with the consequences of high energy costs. Transportation businesses are energy businesses. The hub-and-spoke system is a geographical solution to an energy cost problem. Both were also responses to excessive regulation. The old commercial airlines were the product of the ancient regime of government that granted route monopolies. Like the phone company, they held their customers hostage. Service was slow and surly. Unions dominated the labor-management equation, adding labor cost fire to the energy cost fuel. Even after airline deregulation (a rare Carter improvement), the old dinosaurs simply could not learn to dance. Southwest was a mammal, however, and perfectly adapted to the new environment.

FedEx is a similar story. It arose as a challenge to a de facto government monopoly—the post office. Many wondered aloud whether such package delivery was even legal. It was found to be so, and an alternative to the long lines and even longer breaks at the post office was created. And they came to you, right to your house. If you didn't know how to fill out the packing slip, the FedEx guy did it for you. It was like spending decades in France begging for service from snooty clerks and then being magically transported to an American Nordstrom's. Ah, the joys of being served.

The technology revolution of the 1970s is more a matter of a shortage of human resources than of natural ones. Labor costs were rising rapidly, along with everything else. High payroll taxes imposed an additional wedge between employers and employees. Falling educational standards made the available and expensive workers less productive. Bill Bennett's special report on education summed up the implications in its neat little title: "A Nation at Risk."

Computers were the solution. Because we see the situation from a vantage point thirty years later, we think of computers as sources of employment. The 1970s saw them as sources of unemployment. The unions bitterly complained about automation. The old anti-steam folk song "The Legend of John Henry" made a comeback on the working-class voice of Johnny Cash. Computers replaced people. Not just people with slide rules, but quasi-professional draftsmen and skilled machinists and semiskilled assembly-line workers. The calculator is a substitute for an innumerate retail clerk as well as a supplement to a financial analyst. Spreadsheets don't replace bookkeepers entirely, but you sure don't need as many to do the same work.

I should know; I was one of them. I graduated from business school and hit the job market in the 1980s, as a newly minted staff accountant for a Big Six accounting firm. I remember my first week on the job, learning to use a "ten-key"—that is, an adding machine. As one walked through the cubicle hives of the twenty-ninth floor of One Oxford Center, you would hear nothing but the chink, chink, chink, chunk of the digit and enter keys and the occasional zhip, zhip, zhip when the final result was printed. If you got one wrong, you redid the whole series. If you needed to change a scenario . . . start again. There must be a better way, I thought. I had been reading George Gilder's *Wealth and Poverty*, in which he predicted that information technology would inevitably lead to leaps in professional productivity similar to those that resulted from heavy machinery's introduction into the labor economy.

I threw myself into learning whatever I could about the computers that were sitting largely unused in the computer lab down the hall. Eventually, I ran across a new spreadsheet program called Lotus 1-2-3 and immersed myself in that, too. It wasn't long before I was the spreadsheet guru, which the partners didn't care about one whit. Until I was given an assignment that in past years had routinely taken at least one week of billed staff accountant work in order to get the numbers rearranged in such a way as to yield useful information for the calculations the client needed. The partner gave me the project and told me to please try to get it done in a week.

I was back in his office that same afternoon. The work was done, checked, and double-checked. The bosses were sold. They had me do a training session every week thereafter to find new productivity gains for the whole office. Compaq portables started appearing in the overhead budgets and shortly thereafter on the desks of the department members.

We were expensive. The education system was churning out a pretty inferior product even when it came to reading and writing, but for math-literate professions, things were even worse. There was a bidding war for guys like me, guys who were good with numbers, knew the financial accounting model, and got good enough grades for a top firm. If we could increase our productivity, enormous labor cost pressures would be removed from a profession that was almost all salary to begin with. The guy who slaved away at creating Lotus might not have known why his product sold so briskly, but it was macroeconomics. Wage inflation was his biggest promoter.

Ditto for the guys who designed those 286 chips that powered the Compaq portable computers sitting on the desks of our best guys. Yes, you need big mathematically talented brains to design the chips. But you don't need them to run the machines. A few highly skilled anomalous math geeks made very good money designing technology that would double and even triple the productivity of the public school masses. I doubt that technology would have emerged so quickly in the 1970s if America had more flexible labor markets and better schools.

Of course, the tax climate helped to midwife the entrepreneurial boom, as well.

Talent had already been driven away to some degree from any part of the economy that depended on traditional capital markets. If you were smart and ambitious and good at math in the late 1960s, there was a good chance that you went to Wall Street. Or maybe you went to work for a big firm that was traded there. But by the mid-1970s, the investors had wised up and were avoiding stock investments. High capital gains tax rates took a risky environment and turned it into a toxic one. The fact that these rates were not adjusted for inflation made it even worse. Of course, indexing capital gains tax rates for inflation had not been much of an issue during previous low-inflation decades, but with the unexpected price surges that came from excessive money creation, all of a sudden capital gains investing became a suckers' bet.

A smart and creative guy with an 800 math SAT score would probably have gone to work for IBM in the 1970s if the economic climate had been better in corporate America. But the climate was lousy and corporate life unappealing, and so Gates and Jobs and an entire generation of top talent went into their various garages and dreamed up the next big thing. The point here is that the icy headwinds that came from the Left and blew through the traditional business enclaves blew these young men toward entrepreneurship.

As I have said elsewhere in this book, I feel the need to stop here and admonish you not to romanticize this. It is a bad thing when a people's rulers smother their economy. Some, as we've described, manage to survive because they have the talent or the guts, or maybe because, for His own unsearchable reasons, the Good Lord has put them in the right place at the right time for success. But the vast majority of people stand at the corporate grindstone, or even worse, at the window of the mill, looking in, waiting for a position. Entrepreneurs are the exception in times like the 1970s and the period we have just entered. I wrote this book so you could be the exception. But I would greatly prefer a business climate where prosperity is the normal course for all.

Here is how to be an exception:

Barack Obama promised, during the campaign, to create a zero percent capital gains tax rate for "small business start-ups." Even if he keeps this promise, this provision will have minimal economic impact on the country in general. But for a small number of people who understand the ways in which tax policy affects financial and economic conditions, the impact is profound.

The Obama proposal to tax small business start-ups at a zero percent capital gains rate is a political gimmick. It will have little economic growth impact. Most small business start-ups are sold once in a lifetime or not at all. The turnover rate is infinitesimally small. From hot dog vendors through body shops up to auto dealers, these businesses tend to be held for the long term. So, although the universe of small businesses is rather large, the universe of small business sales transactions is very small. And let's remember that it is only start-ups that have been mentioned as part of this proposal. This limits the number of firms substantially and the number of transactions even more substantially. If further conditions are imposed (environmental, unionist, and so on), then the universe shrinks yet again.

But if he keeps that promise it may have a major impact on your investment and entrepreneurial decision-making process.

THE POINT OF this section is to alert you to ways in which you might find yourself among that small number of entrepreneurs (or their investors) who use the proposal to advantage.

First, defer your final decision about the structure of your start-up until after we know the details of the proposal. Now is a great time to start a business, but exactly what structure should it have? There are sole proprietorships with no legal status separate from the owner at all. There are Subchapter S corporations and LLCs, both of which create a separate legal entity but are treated as an extension of the individual owner for tax purposes. There are traditional C-companies, which are legally separate and taxed separately, as well. As a general rule (for specifics, talk to your CPA or your tax attorney), the more separate the company is from you, the more legal protection you get for yourself. But also, generally, the more separate it is from you, the fewer the tax advantages.

Second, once you know which structures are eligible for zero percent capital gains treatment, you should structure the financing of your business in such a way as to minimize its short-run profit and maximize its long-run value. You see, under Obama, profit is starting to be taxed more heavily. Most successful small businesses generate more than the $250,000 in profit that pushes the owner into the disfavored caste of "rich." Those who opt to have their companies taxed at the corporate level will also be hit. Obama has pledged to keep corporate tax rates the same, but he and his proxies have threatened to close "loopholes." "Loophole" is left-ese for "business deductions that I don't like." I recently debated Jared Bernstein (now chief economist for Vice President Biden), and he acknowledged that Obama would end some deductions, but added no details. Senator Claire McCaskill on CNBC mentioned depreciation and amortization as examples of corporate loopholes. This is a very strange argument, since depreciation and amortization are seen by most economists as unfavorable to business. You see, the natural way to tax businesses would be to allow them to deduct the money they spend on business equipment in the year in which they spend it. That would be a sensible way to calculate the profit for that year. But the IRS, with a few exceptions, forces the companies to defer deductions over a period of several years. When this is done for physical assets like heavy equipment, it's called "depreciation"; when this is done for intellectual assets like a patent, it's called "amortization." Neither depreciation nor amortization schedules are indexed for inflation; therefore, the company never gets to deduct the full expense of the purchase. The worse the inflation, the worse the problem. If I'm right that we have entered a period of stagflation, then the depreciation problem would be quite significant. The FedEx founder, Fred Smith, has pointed to this as a challenge, even during a phase of tame inflation.

As I said to Mr. Bernstein, if you keep tax rates the same and eliminate certain deductions, you have increased the taxes of the targeted business. So, corporate profits are going to be taxed more heavily at exactly the moment when certain forms of business income (namely, capital gains of small start-ups) are going to be plunging to zero. This means a tremendous opportunity to reduce taxes by shifting income from one category to another. This must be part of the design of any entrepreneurial start-up that might qualify for zero percent capital gains treatment.

The effect is huge. Income taxed at the top individual level will top out at least at 40 percent, and there will likely be substantial increases in Social Security and Medicare taxes. The top effective combined federal rate could easily be 50 percent—or, by planning your business in such a way as to minimize its profit and maximize its value, you can sell that business for a capital gains rate of zero percent. The spread between being taxed at 50 percent and not at all is large enough for me to recommend that you throw out the traditional principle of business management that says transactions have to make business sense before they make tax sense. Under Obamanomics, tax costs trump most other costs of doing business.

## M&A Is the New IPO

The role previously played by initial public offerings (IPOs) will increasingly by played by mergers and acquisitions (M&A). That is because there is another principle of sound business policy that is distorted under the new taxtopia: building a company to last. The age-old model for entrepreneurs is summed up well in the title of the great business book *Built to Last*. The opposite strategy is summed up well in the title of the famous article "Built to Flip." During the dot-com boom, many entrepreneurs built companies that were designed not to last but to be flipped; that is, sold to a larger company. And in a world with a 5,000 basis-point spread (that is, fifty full percentage points' difference) between ordinary income tax rates and a zero percent capital gains tax rate for start-ups, the build-to-flip strategy will make a comeback.

For example: Don't build one big company that does five things well. Build five different small companies, *seriatim*, and sell each of them in order to a larger one at zero percent capital gains tax. I have two close friends who are both highly successful entrepreneurs. One has created ten businesses, and most were successful. He sold each successful business, and then moved on to start another one. My other friend has built one large business, which he built from scratch to over one thousand employees. This friend once said to me, "I'm not that much different from Rob; I also keep starting new businesses, I just call them all Fred's Installations." By this he meant that he reinvented his business every five years or so, but he just never changed buildings or names or signs or key employees or corporate structure. One business reinventing itself ten times is not really that different from one man taking his key players from one business to another ten times.

But imagine how that would change under Obama. Fred would be paying what amounts to roughly 40 percent of his profit to the IRS. Of the remaining 60 percent, the IRS would take almost half of what the company distributes to him in dividends and/or salary. That 50 percent of 60 percent is 30 percent, so 30 percent of his hard-earned profit goes into his pocket, while 70 percent goes to the tax man.

Rob, on the other hand, built high-tech start-ups, which didn't really make any money for several years. He prides himself on not ever taking a paycheck from his companies. He would pay a minimal corporate income tax on his small tech earnings and nothing at all when he sells to someone else. Fred pays 70 percent, Rob pays maybe 10 or 15 percent in those minority of years in which he makes a profit. Under Obama it pays to be a Rob and doesn't pay to be a Fred.

Of course, I could stop here to deliver a little homily about how this tax-inspired market distortion probably puts more instability into labor markets. When a big company buys a little one, that's almost never a cause for celebration around the water cooler, except for the few key guys who have equity in the deal. The build-to-flip strategy creates lots of risky ventures that simply don't make sense on their own if they are never purchased. So there are a significant number of companies that will simply crash and burn; all the employees will be laid off. Think Pets.com. If, on the other hand, the little company is purchased, market power is concentrated in the big company that buys it. The acquiring company will have used its cash advantage to buy even more market share for itself. Furthermore, income inequality, that dread of the Left, will be increased because the build-to-flip model is often financed through private equity venture capital funds in which only the wealthy are legally allowed to participate. Only the very rich are able to cash in on tax-free venture capital. I'll leave the rest of the homily about liberal hypocrisy to someone else. You are here to prosper under the current market distortions, not gripe about them; at least until the next national election.

Be a Rob. When you have a new idea, start a new company. Create a new corporate entity. Move the most appropriate people from your current venture to the new venture.

Divide your time between them. Be meticulous about keeping the funding separate from each other. Use your losses from the new company to offset your gains from the main company, decreasing your tax bill. Consult your tax advisor on all the details about this.

Probably the best guy in the country when it comes to understanding this new world is Jon Fisher, a serial entrepreneur and the author of *Strategic Entrepreneurism*. Jon's model is to create businesses precisely in order for them to be acquired.

According to Fisher, in order to increase your probability of selling to someone else, you need to design your new company the right way from the beginning. You need to know the sort of company you will want to be purchased by and put your company in its way. For this, focus on a problem they have to which you have the solution. Large companies have a lot of trouble encouraging innovation in their ranks. Few are able to break the culture of bureaucracy and replace it with a culture of agility. Often the worst problem solvers stay and work the system, while the best leave in frustration. If you are that guy, the time may be right. If you know that guy (from your neighborhood, church, kids' soccer league, and so on), you may have a partner. Frequently, technical people are as mystified by finance as we financial guys are by their gizmos. That's good. That's opportunity.

Strategic entrepreneurialism, you may note, is not the typical "follow your bliss" approach to entrepreneurship. It is not "find something that you really want to do and then do it better than anyone else and the money will follow."

Save that schlock for commencement speeches.

This is more like: find something that someone else really wants you to do, and do it so well that he will need to buy you out for great big buckets of money. After that you can follow your bliss.

You need one more thing before the sale: After you've solved the problem, you need to catch the whale. You need to procure the client that your target company wants, so that the target company has to buy you in order to get that client. In other words, you have to compete against the big boy and win, and then sell out to him. In order to do this, you need to look for an environment in which you have the advantage.

What advantages might a start-up have over a behemoth? Perhaps you've got the secret sauce, the better product that the big guys don't have. Don't count on a secret sauce strategy. Big companies have huge research and development budgets, staffed with Caltech guys shackled by impregnable noncompete agreements. You can't just hire the guy who thought up Post-it Notes while on 3M's payroll and corner the market. 3M owns that guy.

The frustrated engineer who leaves before the big discovery might be a better ticket. He's certainly more motivated. Technical guys tend to be straight salary. His salary is the same if he invents the Flowbee (a vacuum cleaner attachment that cuts hair, you know, as seen on TV) or the Flux Capacitor time-travel device.

So, the technical staff is not highly motivated, because they're on fixed salary. Of course, the sales staff is probably not on fixed salary. The sales guy who harpoons the whale will eat well. He's hungry, but he only knows how to sell the stuff that already exists. He lacks the skill set to compete effectively with an entrepreneur. It doesn't pay for him to think up new products that will never be produced. In order to compete with the entrepreneur, he would have to make two sales: one to his employer ("You need to build a time machine") and another to the big client ("Yes, it really works. Here's tomorrow's newspaper"). And, of course, he is competing with other salesmen in his own company. No, he'll stick with Widget, Son of Widget, and Widget Goes Hawaiian.

Only the entrepreneur has the incentive and flexibility to get the Flux Capacitor built and sold to the big client whom everyone wants.

Now how to do it: Things may go better if your prospective client is a self-made man. A guy who got to the CEO's chair by playing it safe and never getting voted off the island is not your most promising prospect. He doesn't take risks; no one ever got fired for hiring IBM and all of that. The self-made man is not stupid. He won't make a deal with you that doesn't make sense for him, but he'll give another entrepreneur a fair shot. Call early in the morning, before the staff is in. Even if you end up leaving a message, he'll know what time you called. Be in your office ready to take his return call early, as well; otherwise, it's a gimmick, and guys like that can see through gimmicks.

This is how the new fortunes are going to be made. Initial public offerings (IPOs) are basically extinct on American soil. They were wiped out in the 2002 regulatory massacre known as Sarbanes-Oxley. The burden of compliance with a far more expensive regulatory state is manageable for a big company that can amortize this and other overhead costs over a very wide revenue base. But a little guy doesn't have the same economies of scale. I've been on the board of at least one small publicly traded company that decided to delist itself in order to shed those costs. It basically cost us an extra million a year to be publicly traded, and we were small enough that we genuinely felt the loss of that million. Many companies went private after Sarbox. Many companies that would otherwise have made their shares available to the general public stayed closely held. The central planners are likely to get tougher, not friendlier, under Obama. The credit crisis, and the Madoff scandal, and all the other scandals real and imagined that emerge in the wake of tough economic times provide ample pretext for a more draconian financial architecture.

It always works that way; scandals come in waves. After the Enron scandal, my friend Brian Wesbury asked me whether I thought there would be more. I said there would. "Every audit manager in every accounting firm is going to get the same question from the firm partners this month," I told him. "Do we have any clients who might turn out to be another Enron?" So they sent their staff accountants down to the file room to pull a dozen or more sets of audit working papers and began to look for the next Enron. They found WorldCom, Tyco, Global Crossing, and a host of others.

The same thing will happen to any firm that bears even the slightest resemblance to Madoff's, or any of the other real or manufactured scandals that will make headlines in this climate of being tough on business. And when they are found, the momentum will build for more laws and more fines. Never mind that Madoff, and Ken Lay, and the rest of the corporate crooks were violating already existing laws, and that many of them tended to closely align themselves with the leading voices for more regulation. Madoff, for example, was a major donor to some of the chief congressional voices for more regulation and an advisor to former SEC chairman Arthur Levitt, who has been one of the most vocal proponents for regulation. All of this has been forgotten and more Sarboxes have been called for, and are being brought into existence.

That's not the kind of soil in which to plant IPOs. Add to that mix the fact that investment banks, the traditional under-writers of new offerings, are flat on their backs for the time being, and you have an intensely hostile environment. Mergers and acquisitions are the workaround to this problem. Risk-traumatized companies are sitting on large piles of hoarded cash. It made sense during a credit crunch, which is also a deflationary cycle. Cash, at times like those, is king. Smart players hold their money, which gets more valuable by the minute, and wait for deflating prices to bottom out. But when the money starts flowing again, inflation picks up, and then firms are in a hurry to buy before the prices rise. They're in a hurry to trade less and less valuable dollars for more and more valuable investments. That's your moment. But in the past you would have gone to an investment bank. Now you go to a conventional company. They're the new bank. Microsoft is the bank. Oracle is the bank. Google is the bank. Bank of America? Not the bank: no money, no confidence. The new NASDAQ is the acquiring company. Being acquired is the new IPO.

Plan your company that way from the beginning. Plan it so that you can get your income at as close to a zero percent tax rate as possible. The way to do that is to plan your company so that the value it creates is captured in the form of enhanced sales price rather than enhanced operating profit.

This means reinvesting revenues into assets that increase the net value of the company without increasing profit margins. Businesses with cash-flow, as opposed to accrual, accounting have an advantage here, since they find it easier to deduct their expenses up front. Businesses whose expenditures are not subject to depreciation rules, which force them to defer their tax write-offs, are similarly attractive. A business that buys heavy equipment and uses it over the next ten years to produce a product on which it is forced to declare a profit early is not "built to flip." A business that builds strong brand value through immediately deductible advertising expenditures, and which runs at break even right up until the time it can be sold to a larger competitor who can financially exploit its goodwill and intellectual capital, is ideal from the standpoint of the build-to-flip strategy.

These accounting and tax-planning issues are highly complex and will evolve as the administration writes the regulations regarding its zero capital gains rate for start-ups. So the tactics will undoubtedly change, but the principle remains the same: Shift income from ordinary profit to capital gains to minimize taxes.

## Angels and Profits

What if you do not want to start a business? Perhaps you are retired or involved with a highly demanding career and are just looking for a place to put the money that you earn from your day job. Maybe you're just not wired to start businesses. Most people aren't.

You can still find wealth-creating opportunities in entrepreneurship even if you are not the entrepreneur. You can invest in small start-up companies. Don't worry; you didn't waste your time reading the previous entrepreneurially focused sections. They will help you choose which businesses to invest in. And if your method of investing includes investor input, you can use the insights gleaned above in order to guide the business in which you have placed your hard-earned money.

If you are a person of high net worth and you don't want to actually run a small business, I'd like you to consider something called "angel investing." Angel investors (or "angels," for short) are individuals who make substantial investments in businesses that are too large to be funded by the founder but too small to be of interest to venture capitalists. Typically the founder of a business pays its first expenses. He might use money from a savings account, a severance payment, or a personal credit card. Some go beyond that to friends and family. Though the thresholds vary widely from person to person, typically that method of funding maxes out at one or two hundred thousand dollars.

But what happens after that?

Venture capitalists are almost never interested in anything less than a million dollars, and most are not even interested in the million-dollar deals. Angel investors are the people who fill in that gap. They are the people who get companies from the "friends and family" level to the "venture capital" level. Fathers-in-law are good for the five-figure deals, and the seven-and-up-figure deals are made by venture capital guys in oak-paneled rooms. The six-figure realm is the realm of the angels. And angels are about to get more important than they have been in any of our lifetimes.

The name "angel investor" goes back to the days when struggling Broadway shows were bailed out by wealthy patrons who, though technically stepping in as investors, were in fact performing an act of kindness. In exchange for their largesse, they were praised by the artistic community and, from time to time, got their mistresses good parts in a play. These guys were suckers, not investors. But they were angelic in the sense that they brought good news to people who really needed it. They supplied capital where capital was scarce.

Well, capital is scarce nearly everywhere now, and this means we're in a "buyer's market" for investment in small businesses. The more clogged credit markets are with regulations, mandates, and just plain fear, the more need there is for some sort of alternate financing arrangements. The lower the investee is on the political and financial totem pole, the better the deal is for the investor. This does not in any way cancel the need for extremely diligent research and a high degree of selectivity. You're looking for very promising low-risk businesses that are suffering from credit disruptions for reasons that arise from general credit conditions, not any conditions that are specific to that company. Your job is to stand outside of the nurseries of capitalism with the kind of big nets that catch babies, but not bathwater.

There will be a lot of bathwater. Here's how to spot it: Bathwater investments come from friends and family and have social pressure attached. But the problem is that unless you move in a social environment that is coincidentally inhabited by entrepreneurial geniuses in undervalued sectors, it would be a terribly unlikely coincidence if the best investment ideas for you just happened to be attached to your brother-in-law. Your best policy is to establish a no-friends-and-family policy from the beginning. This is much easier to do if you are part of a larger angel network or some other type of pooled funding. These help you avoid awkward moments at family gatherings. You can just say that you passed along young Josh's business plan for a video-game testing service to the business development committee of your angel network, and they'll be sure to contact him if they need any more information.

Bathwater can also, just now, look like any business idea whose business plan says something like "We expect the economy to return to normal soon, and demand to resume as a result." Economic leftism is the new normal for at least the next several years. No business plan that depends on any other normal is worth the risk.

Bathwater that depends on Internet gimmicks will also likely short out your finances. Forget anything that takes something that already works perfectly well and tries to turn it into a Web site. If you hear this pitch: "It's just like a regular restaurant (dry-cleaning service, hairstylist, or ambulance service) but on the Web," run away. We've gotten all our low-hanging Web-based fruit. When I spend my morning clearing my in-box of e-mails about puppies and random acts of kindness forwarded by nice middle-aged ladies, I think I can safely conclude that Web usage has grown way past the early adopters of Generation Y. The Internet is no longer a gimmick; it is now a tool. Businesses that depend on the newness of the Web are doomed to failure, while businesses that use it as a tool, especially as a cost-cutting tool, have a chance to succeed.

There is probably no greater example of the Internet as cost-cutting tool than media. Newspapers are dropping like flies. Some may actually get government bailouts, which is a howling violation of freedom of the press. To subsidize liberal media and not their conservative competition is to suppress conservative media. This is not a drill; Pennsylvania's governor, Ed Rendell, has been openly cogitating about a bailout for the *Philadelphia Inquirer*. There is also a movement growing that would treat big-city newspapers as objects of philanthropy. Foundations, generally created from the wealth of long-gone religious, conservative men, are looking at making contributions to foundering newspapers. Let them do it. Let the papers become the captives of the lefty trust-fund class. This will make newspapers less responsive to the middle class, and they will lose market share as they tilt their coverage more and more to please a few thousand privileged liberal elites. Blogs are a high-risk investment, so if you buy some interest in alternative media such as this, it goes in the most risk-tolerant portion of your portfolio. But once there, it is a promising area.

Local news coverage is the next frontier of Internet journalism. This is especially worth investigating in cities with only one, always liberal, newspaper. A little money will go a long

way in buying services from a few conservative stringer reporters and a young guy who can get their work posted quickly.
Lots of reporters are getting laid off, and it's more often a
matter of seniority than of competence. They'll work cheap.
Find the one in a hundred who deviates from the dominant
liberal ideology (I bet those guys get laid off faster than the liberal ones), and pay him per piece written. Build alliances with
conservative talk radio. Get advertisers from the pool of people
who have been treated unfairly by the newspaper. You'll find
quite a few of them.

Bathwater that depends on government appropriations is
just too murky to be of any use. Unless you are a political in-
sider, you are ill equipped to chase the subsidies. A man can
make a great deal of money this way, but it is a lifetime occupa-
tion, and it's as specialized as brain surgery, if not as beneficial
to the body politic. This is for guys who go to all the fund-
raisers and know the candidate and most of his staff and—more
important—are known by them. It's for people who know the
appropriations and procurement processes so well that they can
navigate them in their sleep. Watching Chris Matthews lean in
and raise his voice on *Hardball* and scanning the *Washington Post*
are not nearly enough to get you through this world.

We're done with the bathwater. Now: What do babies look
like?

Babies are businesses that can function well in the new era
of stagnation. This is a different environment than in the recent
past. Several years ago, I interviewed an author of a book about
millionaires under the age of thirty. At first I wondered what
the difference was between them and other successful entrepreneurs. As I read example after example it became perfectly clear
what the common theme was—these businesses were all catering to unprecedented opulence. The new success stories were

gourmet breads, coffees, and candies. Personal services on image consulting, dress, and physical and emotional development were the road to riches for Generation Y. I realized that the advantage these kids had was that they were willing to launch businesses providing goods and services that no sane person of *my* generation (born in 1962) would think normal people would be willing to pay for. We walk our own darn dogs, and are shocked that anybody else would pay someone to do it. I grew up in a world bookended by two plausible economic scenarios, the stagflation of my high school years and the tech boom of my late thirties. My normal was between these two. But my kids grew up in a world sandwiched between the tech boom and a mild recession in 2000–2001, which makes dog-walking and image-consulting services the normal for them. On the other end of the spectrum, my grandparents grew up in a world sandwiched between the Great Depression and the relatively small boom following World War II. That was their normal.

For a while, at least, our normal is going to be one of slow growth and troublesome levels of inflation. That means that unless the community being served is made up of lobbyists or alternate energy mavens, Sally's Spa of Decadence is not a promising business.

Sally's discount food outlet, however, might be. Sally's low-cost garden supplies might be, as well. Trade schools are a natural choice in scary times. People tend to turn what was formerly downtime into self-education time. Expect less interest in cute kids on the way back from the dentist on YouTube and more interest in how to use Microsoft Excel, or even how to grow soybeans in your front yard. This will be (heck, already is) an era of enormous economic anxiety. The president will not assuage that anxiety; he will stoke it and harness it for his own political ends. Much of America will respond to him in exactly the way he hopes. They will sign up for free health care for their kids and later for themselves. They will arrange their lives in whatever way is needed to get the refunds, refundable credits, and subsidies. Washington will herd them in directions that Washington chooses, and they will follow.

But many will not follow. They will stubbornly hold on to their own health savings accounts and 401(k)s. They will educate their children in private schools or at home. They will continue to educate themselves with books, how-to videos, software manuals, and educational software. They'll listen to smart talk radio (what there is of it) and watch smart talk TV (what there is of that). If things get bad enough, they'll garden, fish, and hunt. In fact, even if things don't get that bad, they'll learn (or relearn) those things, just to be sure. Instead of being afraid, they'll be busy.

You are going to look for opportunities to invest in the businesses that help that group of people. You're not going to capitalize on human misery. You're not going to start a Rent-a-TV center. You're going to look at things like low-cost garden supplies and training. You're going to look at hunting and fishing supplies and training. Perhaps someone will start a school teaching people how to do small-engine repair. I have a friend who repairs old stereos and sells them on eBay. So far, he's been recession-proof. Firing ranges look like the kind of business that helps alleviate fear in times of trouble. Lots of people are buying guns right now, which is more than a little scary. How many of them are getting real first-rate training in gun safety? Market this program to the wives and mothers. Don't underestimate the fear out there. Don't scold it and don't demean it. Help alleviate it. If people are running the worst-case scenario in their heads, give them the urban gardening knowledge, or hunting and fishing knowledge, that they need. Sell it to them cheap. Sell them the seeds and the chickens and coops that they need to feel secure. Even if the worst does not occur, are they really worse off for having spent their evenings learning how to fix a chain saw than they would be if they had spent their evenings watching *American Idol*, or worse, the aforementioned Mr. Matthews?

Prestige private education might not be at the top of our list for a while, either. I think that Americans are going to ask harder and harder questions about the cost-benefit analysis of a high-grade liberal arts education for the time being. The old argument for liberal arts as opposed to vocational education was that the former made one well rounded. The idea is that you wanted your electrical engineers to still be familiar with the classics. The problem is that the liberal arts professors spend most of their time pissing on the classics that the marketing departments dangle in front of the parents. You might send your kids to college to get Shakespeare and Austen. And they will get them: your kids will see the greats of English literature vivisected before their eyes. Shakespeare's texts are tortured into confessing to anti-Semitism, patriarchy, and jingoism. Austen witch-trials elicit revelations of repressed homoeroticism, and so on. Formerly oblivious parents are beginning to catch on. That's why religious schools are growing so much more quickly than secular ones. But what happens when the parents find out that with very few exceptions, the prestigious religious schools, whose non-ivied halls are filled with professors who studied under the same postmodern lefties, are not fundamentally different in curriculum from the secular ones? Maybe in an age of abundance, they'd grit their teeth and sign the checks. In an age of stagflation, not so much.

Low-cost alternatives to traditional education will boom. Small and inexpensive schools for all ages are a promising business. Many are based in preexisting affinity groups: churches, synagogues, chambers of commerce, and fraternal organizations. They are skill- and knowledge-focused, not credit-focused. These are good business models and they don't need much capital to start, but they may need some to expand. This is a good opportunity for angel investors.

Another way to recognize babies (as opposed to bathwater) is that they look like adults, only smaller. They do what the big guys do, only cheaper. You are looking for products and services that undercut, through lower overhead and nonexistent legacy costs, established services. You are, therefore, looking for businesses that are not subject to economies of scale. You don't want to be competing with Walmart or Microsoft. But you may be able to compete with a giant accounting, finance, law, or computer consulting firm, which must rent high-cost downtown office space in order to keep up appearances. They need the oak on the wall; it says, "We're still rich; we're still the best, and that's why you pay us so much." The $200 wing tips and $1,000 suits say the same thing.

The problem is that the clients know they're paying for oak and leather and glass-paneled elevators that you can't get on until you've signed in with security and gotten your lapel badge. These things, along with marquee corporate titles, have now become negative-value brands. The smart consumer is looking for respectable but affordable.

When smart consumers are out shopping for professional services like law or finance, what will they be looking for? They'll be looking for people who are smart, hungry, and not the ones who were in charge when things went so horribly wrong in our economy.

But the smart and hungry up-and-comers are anathema to bank loan officers, who are parsing out their capital with Prufrockian coffee spoons in ways least likely to get them in hot water with Congress. Bankers toss out entire bins of applications for small business start-ups and ongoing finance loans, even the genuinely promising ones.

Get your nets ready; there are some million-dollar babies being thrown away in those bins.

I suggest, however, that at least in the beginning you don't try to do this on your own. Angel investors, like their celestial namesakes, seem to do their best work in hosts. Some angel groups are very loose-knit, basically matching services. An entrepreneur approaches the group and submits a business plan. The information is passed around and any member is free to follow up and take a closer look at the opportunity. The main thing is that each investor invests individually. Even if more than one member of the group puts money into the deal, they are all distinct investors, who cut their own checks.

Sometimes these angel investor groups have a central support staff, paid for by fees from the investors in the network. The idea is to take advantage of some economies of scale and still keep individual autonomy. Groups like this function basically like a club or a professional association. The "dues" go to pay the salary of an executive director and perhaps a small staff. Their job is to do the "due diligence" that is required in any investment. That is, they check the references and credit history. Look over the financial statements and any audit reports there might be. The staff is the "tire kicking" and "oil gauge checking" operation. There's no sense in each of thirty different investors doing those same things individually—it's redundant to do so.

Once the due diligence has been done, the investment is still a financial "jump ball." Any investor can go for it, and that investor is on his own. These loose networks are strong on individual autonomy, but short on risk sharing. Certain types of investors love this aspect of it. Many angel investors are former entrepreneurs, who have sold their own businesses and are sitting around, bored, on top of big piles of money. They want the adrenaline.

Other angel investors are successful corporate executives or professionals. They are not risk junkies. They worked their way steadily up the corporate hierarchy, or through law (or medical) school, and then up through their practice. They want to make money, but they aren't looking for thrills or micromanagement opportunities. They are, however, looking to learn more about investing. They also feel uncomfortable putting all of their money into gigantic publicly traded companies, where they have no genuine input at all.

This latter category of angel—doctors, lawyers, executives—are far more interested in pooling their money to spread the risk. In this model, not only do they share the information that comes from the central office, but they collectively decide whether to invest. By joining their capital together this way, they can also diversify their investments. If a tenth of your money goes into a shopping mall, that means there are another nine-tenths that can go into nine other similarly large investments. Your initial investment goes into a big pot, and from that big pot it is parceled out to the most promising capital seekers.

The legal structure of these various pots varies quite a bit. Sometimes the angel network is a partnership or a private corporation. Sometimes the central office is employed by a nonprofit or a professional association. The structure varies, but the basic model is the same—private investments in small business on a scale that permits actual human contact between investor and entrepreneur.

Angel investors are almost always what the regulators call "qualified investors," which means they've got at least a million dollars and a few hundred thousand dollars a year in income. This varies with marital status, so talk to your advisor to make sure you're qualified.

I mentioned above that I believe the credit crisis in which we find ourselves is conducive to angel investing, precisely because it is not conducive to traditional bank financing. The need for capital does not disappear just because the political class becomes hostile to capital deployment. In fact, the political disruptions of credit markets that we've seen in recent years have caused credit shortages, panics, and therefore even greater shortages. The world becomes more capital-hungry the more capital is withheld. This tilts the table to the advantage of the angel investor, who can largely take his pick and dictate his terms. However, this new environment requires a new kind of angel investor. Angel investors, in the past, have acted like venture capital Mini-Mes. That is, they have funded tech firms, software, hardware, radical new models. Like the venture capital crowd, they've risked losing their investment in most of the start-ups in the hope of getting a "ten bagger" somewhere in the mix. You can lose it all on most firms, but if you get a tenfold return on a couple of them, you still make money. But the new angel investor is replacing the dysfunctional bank more than he's replacing the venture capitalist. This means that he must adjust his risk level. It's okay to fund a dry-cleaning place, or an auto dealership. It's okay to get a solid local business through a credit crunch with an injection of equity capital. The new angel investors set out for a zero failure track record, just like the bank. Yes, it's okay to buy a piece of "the next big thing," but don't buy ten next big things.

The current mood of left-wing economic populism creates an additional advantage for the angel investor over and against other forms of lightly regulated capital: it makes the business environment comparatively more favorable for small than for large businesses. When the Left dons the mask of populism, it finds itself prevented by its own carefully crafted image from attacking the smallest businesses. In order to convince the electorate that they're not against business, just against big business, they have to leave the little guy alone. They have to set a tax bar fairly low for very small businesses. They have to exempt them from most of the regulatory maze of unions, health care, and environmental mandates. This makes certain classes of businesses less hampered than their large competitors, but, ironically, less able to get financing.

This makes the field in which the angels keep watch by night both promising and highly profitable.

*Gloria In Excelsis Deo.*


## Act Globally

Ronald Reagan's favorite joke was about the kid who came down the stairs on Christmas morning and saw a huge pile of droppings. He yelped with glee, ran over to the pile, and began digging through it with his bare hands. His parents asked, "What are you doing, son?"

He said, "When I saw the pile of manure, I thought, there must be a pony here somewhere."

So here's the manure:

When the Obama apologists say they are only raising income taxes back to the rates they were at during Bill Clinton's administration or the capital gains tax rates back to the levels they were at under Ronald Reagan, they are in fact showering you with, well, pony (or bull) by-product. It's not that there is no element of truth in this assertion. The statutory levels being proposed are, in fact, the same as those in the Clinton era, although far larger numbers of people are at those top rates than were there in 1993. And furthermore, Obama is eliminating many deductions in those brackets, which amounts to the same effect as would result from rates higher than Clinton's. And, to add injury to the previous insult that was added to the previous injury, Obama is raising the cap on Social Security payroll taxes to levels far above the Clinton levels. And, as for Reagan, he reluctantly traded a higher capital gains rate for a lower income tax rate toward the end of his administration.

But the biggest piece of manure is the context of global competitiveness. When Clinton raised rates in 1993, the dust from the falling Berlin Wall had not yet settled. Socialist or social democrat regimes ran every major developed economy in the world. The environment around the world was still intensely hostile to investment. America could get away with a 40 percent tax rate in a world where 70 percent rates were still common.

But those rates aren't common anymore. After almost two decades of aggressive tax- and regulation-cutting around the globe, America is no longer at the top of the competitive list. Sarbanes-Oxley (outlined earlier in this book) has placed us at a tremendous disadvantage to other financial centers, such as London and Dubai. And the United States is probably, all things considered, taxing businesses at higher tax rates than any other developed country. When Clinton moved the top individual tax rate to 40 percent, Ukraine was little more than a former industrial wasteland. Now they've got a 20 percent flat tax. So does most of the rest of Eastern Europe. Ireland is a low-tax Celtic tiger. The arena is incomparably tougher than it was in the '70s, '80s, and '90s. Gentleman Jimmy Braddock was a heck of a fighter in his day, but if you clone him and put him in the ring with Mike Tyson, you'd better have an ambulance ready. The modern world is far too tough and competitive now to raise the cost of doing business in the United States when it's being cut everywhere else. Capital is now more mobile than it has been at any time in history. You can move it with the click of a mouse.

The manure is: The new tax rates will drive a large pool of mobile capital out of America. The pony is that you can move your capital out of the country the same as anybody else can. Indian investors can flee U.S. capital markets, but so can U.S. investors. You are free, legally, morally, and technologically, to invest outside of your country of origin. Former Citigroup chairman Walter Wriston said, "Capital goes where it is welcome, and stays where it is well treated." There's a time when that only applied to the big guys. Now it is more true of the little guy. As predicted, the meek have inherited the earth. Any skeptical Japanese housewife can watch Bernanke on YouTube, mutter "Kobe dung" under her breath, and sell dollars and buy yen. So can you.

So the issue at hand is where to put your money. I use the word "where" geographically, not rotationally. I'm not saying "put your money in plastics." I'm saying put your money in India. And I really do mean India, not China, and not Russia, either. To understand why, you're going to need to understand something that hedge fund managers have dubbed the J-Curve.

The J-Curve, popularized in a book of the same name, is a way of visually representing the relationship between freedom and stability. It helps investors get a sense of the amount of risk in a given country. As in most graphs, the up-and-down arrow represents one variable and the right-to-left arrow represents a related one. The J-shaped curve represents the relationship between the two variables in any given instance.

In this case, the up-and-down line (Algebra 2 flashback: it's called the y-axis) represents the level of stability. The left-to-right line represents freedom (in Algebra 2-ese, it's the x-axis). You are used to seeing straight lines that point diagonally up and to the right, or down and to the right, because those kinds of lines represent simple, linear relationships, such as supply of a good increases as sales price does (upward-sloping supply curve) or that demand for the same product falls as price rises (a downward-sloping demand curve). But reality being what it is, it usually serves up more complex relationships than can be easily captured by a straight line. That's why we have curves—to create pictures to help us see relationships that are counterintuitive and dynamic. The Laffer Curve is a great example of this. As tax rates rise, tax revenues rise, too. So far, that would look like an upward-sloping line. But at some point taxes get high enough that the line turns around and goes the other way. People move, cheat, or stop working. Revenues start to fall, until at somewhere around 100 percent tax rates, Uncle Sam gets nothing, the same as he would with tax rates at 0 percent. We can argue endlessly about the shape of the curve and the point beyond which taxes start to cost the government revenues, but the fact of a curve seems unassailable. There is a low rate at which tax revenues must be negligible, and there is a high rate at which they must be, as well. And there is a curve that describes every rate in between those two. It doesn't make sense at first, and most liberals stay at that level of understanding, but over time the counterintuitive reality that countries that exist in the top half of the Laffer Curve will raise revenues by lowering taxes becomes comprehensible and finally intuitively obvious. Just because it's not easy doesn't mean it's not true.

The J-Curve is kind of like that. We have some sort of social studies and *Schoolhouse Rock*–Pavlovian response (reinforced by decades of newspaper editorials) that makes us think that when freedom and democracy increase, we get more of everything good in real time in direct proportion. Since America is a very stable and free democracy (a representative one), we think that if we just push any given country into democracy and freedom, they will increase their stability. The only problems with this view are history and human nature. Iraq became suddenly freer and more democratic, but not suddenly more stable. When the last czar of Russia fell to democratic reformers, they didn't get more stability. They got another revolution, a brutal Bolshevik one. The "democratic revolution" of Iran in 1979 earned them a medieval theocracy.

Examples could be multiplied, and unfortunately have been, but the lesson is simple—when tyrannies lose their grip and the people become freer, they lose stability. When that happens there are only two ways to move toward order—go back to tyranny or go on into a stable freedom. That's why the line eventually curves upward.

This lesson is incredibly important for investors like you and me. It is why in the spring of 2008, when virtually everyone was buzzing about China and its markets and predicting big gains associated with the Beijing Olympics, I suggested rather strongly to the investment committee I chaired at the time that we zero out entirely the China section of our portfolio. China was then, and still is, on the wrong side of the J-Curve, and the Olympics would reveal that fact. I think China may at some point be a great world power and a good place to invest your money, but it has a revolution somewhere in its future, and the smart money buys in after, not before, revolutions.

Russia had its democratic revolution, moving down the J-Curve, then saw the disorder, lost her nerve, and is moving back toward authoritarian rule. She backslid. If she's going to get to freedom and stability, she's going to need to go through another one, so steer clear of the ruble. Forget rising oil prices and all of the other sirens that call from Mother Russia. In the end, every natural resource investment is only as good as the contracts with which it is made. Putin and company are not so big on contracts. Unless you speak the language and know the culture better than whoever you might be buying investments from or in, steer clear of Russia.

So that knocks out two of the countries commonly comprising the emerging market block known as BRIC (Brazil, Russia, India, and China). That leaves half a BRIC for you to invest in, but half a brick is better than none. Let's take a closer look at India.

India has been a functioning representational democracy since 1949. It inherited the King James Bible, the Magna Carta, the Book of Common Prayer, Shakespeare, and the Common Law from Britain. It survived its war for independence and then a devastating jihadist civil war immediately after. It's dealt with a cold war and shared borders with a nuclear Islamic state, and to the north, the world's largest dictatorship. India has had her birth pangs. She still struggles with questions about exactly how capitalist she wants to be, but in the end her representative system and the reality feedback loop that it sets up between socialism and financial pain keeps her from backsliding completely the way other regimes do. India is the biggest opportunity for equity investors looking for good bets on the far side of the J-Curve.

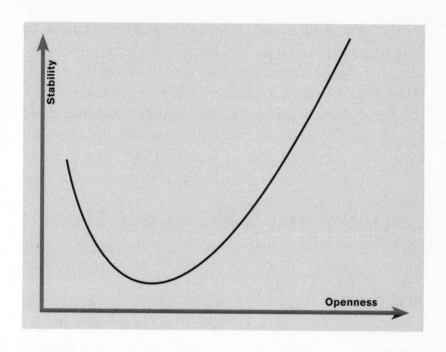

## Acres of Diamonds Strategy

At the same time that you should be expanding your investing horizon globally, you should also be focusing aspects of it more locally. For that you will need the help of Russell Conwell. Russell Conwell is responsible for the most successful business speech in American history. It has come to be known as "Acres of Diamonds," and he delivered it more than six thousand times during his adult life in the early twentieth century. "Acres of Diamonds" was so successful that he raised well in excess of $100 million in current dollars. He used the bulk of this fortune to found Temple University in Philadelphia. Temple is well known, but Conwell is largely forgotten. That's a pity, because the economic message he preached before the great move toward the rise of economic globalization has become pertinent again on the eve of its potential decline.

The core of the speech is a story that he heard from an Arab trader while taking a boat trip in what we now call Iraq. The guide told him the story of a Persian named Ali Hafed. Hafed owned a very large farm in which he lived contentedly and wealthily until one day a traveling priest told him about a great diamond mine in India. The priest told him about the tremendous monetary value of diamonds and the power that such great wealth confers. He told Hafed that with a diamond mine he could buy thrones for his sons.

Hafed was never the same after this conversation. He wanted more than anything to find a diamond mine, and so he sold his farm and traveled the world in search of one. In the end, he died, penniless and distraught, by his own hand.

But the story doesn't end with Hafed. The man to whom Hafed sold his farm one day led his camel to drink from a stream that ran through the property. There he saw a gleam of light reflecting back at him from a black stone jutting out of the water. You've probably guessed the end of the story. The man had just discovered the diamond mine of Golconda, the largest diamond mine in the world.

That story, and the others he collected over the years and added to it, was the source of Conwell's fortune and many other fortunes as well. Some of the great entrepreneurs of his generation started by buying a ticket to hear "Acres of Diamonds."

The message is clear enough. You are more likely to find your fortune at home than abroad. First of all, you know your own home; in fact, that's the problem. People become bored with the place in which they've spent their lives. They know all the things that are wrong with it. They know all the things they've tried to do there and failed at. This causes them to idealize the world they don't know. They want to pull up stakes and go to New York, Washington, or Los Angeles, unless they grew up in one of those places; then they want to pull up stakes and go someplace else. The problem is that every man is at an advantage in his own town and at a disadvantage in any other. It's not just in sports that we can talk meaningfully about a home field advantage. Yes, some people use their hometown up, and it may become necessary for them to go elsewhere, but such a man is unlikely to do well anywhere.

In addition, it is inherently capital-consuming to attempt a geographical solution to your entrepreneurial frustration. The man who pulls up stakes lives off savings as Hafed did. The man who goes to the "big city" meets a throng of men just like him who got there first. Yes, we hear the stories about the girl who moved to Hollywood and became a movie star, or the man who moved to Washington and became a power broker, but we don't know the names of the 99.9 percent who ended up as waitresses or in the mail room.

The typical path to affluence in America is through the auto dealership, dry-cleaning business, regional brokerage firm, or fast-food franchise. These fortunes are generally attached to last names that are very well known within the county and completely unknown a hundred miles away.

Listen to Conwell's advice to a Philadelphia shopkeeper:

> The man over there who said he could not make anything in a store in Philadelphia has been carrying on his store on the wrong principle. Suppose I go into your store tomorrow morning and ask, "Do you know your neighbor A, who lives one square away, at house No. 1240?"
>
> "Oh, yes, I have met him. He deals here at the counter store."
>
> "Where did he come from?"

"I don't know."

"How many does he have in his family?"

"I don't know."

"What ticket does he vote?"

"I don't know."

"What church does he go to?"

"I don't know, and don't care. What are you asking all these questions for?"

If you had a store in Philadelphia, would you answer me like that? If so, then you are conducting your business just as I carried on my father's business in Worthington, Massachusetts. You don't know where your neighbor came from when he moved to Philadelphia, and now don't care. *If you had cared you would be a rich man now.* If you had cared enough about him to take an interest in his affairs, to find out what he needed, you would have been rich.

Anti-wealth political environments intensify this effect for many reasons. First of all, the self-imposed permanent state of energy supply disruption the environmental Left has foisted on the country gives an inherent advantage to any goods or services that do not travel a great distance. As energy prices rise, the transportation portion of the cost of goods sold rises along with them. When the faddishness of locally grown food wears off, the unnecessarily high costs of long-distance transportation remain embedded in the price of imported foods.

In addition, capital market disruption shortens the length of the chain of trust that it takes to participate in global capital markets. As we've discussed before, the erosion of contracts in the form of either outright breach or effective breach through wild currency devaluations necessarily forces business transactions back to handshake distances.

This move back to relational business transactions does not absolutely preclude global commerce, but it does change it. I have a good friend who does a lot of import and export business in central Asia, in a very small country that is a former Soviet satellite state. Since they're well known for monitoring any mention of their little kingdom in Western media, and since my friend would like to continue to do business there, I'll keep their name secret. The government is hostile to Western businessmen, and the culture is unfamiliar with Western rules of commerce. So how is my friend to buy hundreds of tons of concrete or grapes and be assured of delivery? Tribal bonds. He attends their children's weddings and they attend his. They stay in one another's homes, pray together, do favors for one another. I'm helping my friend to help his friends to get a book of poetry published in an English/native language edition. My friend has, in effect, become part of their tribe, and they have become part of his. Any member of their family who failed to honor these business agreements would be an outcast. The price of a broken contract would be a broken village. In a world where contracts are no longer enforced, character and personal bonds of loyalty become the most valuable terms of trade.

I suspect that we will see ethnic and religious affinity groups emerge as a significant factor in global trade in a protectionist world. One can imagine young men importing goods from their elders in the Old Country. The contracts will be enforced not by the World Trade Organization but by a network of babushka aunts with far more power. A young son of Russian immigrants asked me whether he should move to New York and work for a big financial institution. He was a business major, and that seemed like the natural step to him. I counseled against it (which turned out to be better advice than I knew), and told him to strengthen his contacts with his extended family in Russia. What can you import from there to here? What can you export from here to there? Will your Russian network trust you? Can you trust them? The questions I asked him then are even more important now.

Religious affinity groups among Jewish merchants played a key role in the emergence of the global financial architecture. The story of global capitalism could not be told without the name Rothschild. And the name Rothschild would have remained unknown if it weren't for the network of religious and ethnic kinship groups that were created by the Jewish Diaspora across Europe. Eventually the global market became depersonalized and legally formal. But as those formal institutions become increasingly ignored by the Putins of the world, personal, ethnic, and religious ties move to the fore. Now even American presidents treat trade agreements not as legally binding treaties but as expendable fodder for domestic politics. If this continues, we can expect trade to revert to the informal and the personal. An enormous network of Christian missionary institutions has grown over the past century and a half. It is not hard to imagine such a group producing material as well as spiritual wealth.

As overregulation has caused enormous turbulence on Wall Street and in financial capitals around the world, populist politicians have very effectively shifted the blame away from themselves and onto their victims. "Wall Street" is now a term of intense derision. One of the most successful business television programs of all time was Louis Rukeyser's *Wall Street Week*. Would any sane man name a show after Wall Street now other than a satire or a jeremiad? This means that the traditional financial services brands into which untold millions of advertising dollars have been poured have now crashed. I suspect that for many investors the great names of the great banking houses now possess negative value. This is bad news for them and for their shareholders. It is unjust. However, it is also an opportunity for regional entrepreneurs, who now have a chance to reboot financial services and build on the rubble of the crashed national brands. Hometown pride becomes a very important asset when financial centers implode.

The dissolution of national broadcast media outlets helps with this as well. The Internet and DVR are destroying the traditional national television model. iPods and a new generation of cell phone–enabled MP3 players are doing the same for terrestrial radio. The audiences are being broken down into ever smaller grains and the advertising dollars are even now being ground into dust. This means a huge advantage for local radio and television over national. This creates not just an opportunity for media entrepreneurs but for any entrepreneur who sees the future of broadcasting and guides his advertising dollar appropriately.

I'll end this section with the lesson Conwell used to end his speech to his hometown, Philadelphia. Feel free to substitute the name of your town as well.

> To be great at all one must be great here, now, in Philadelphia. He who can give to this city better streets and better sidewalks, better schools and more colleges, more happiness and more civilization, more of God, he will be great anywhere. Let every man or woman here remember, if you wish to be great at all you must begin

where you are and what you are, in Philadelphia, now. He that can give to his city any blessing, he who can be a good citizen while he lives here, he that can make better homes, sits behind the counter or keeps house, whatever be his life, he who would be great anywhere must first be great in his own Philadelphia.

# CHAPTER SIX

# Debt Investment Strategies

## Bonds Prefer Gentlemen

Of course, in an era of broken covenants, bonds are generally not a good place to be. The very word "bond" denotes the moral principle of moral obligation. But the Left sees no moral obligation from debtors to creditors. If the bank makes a loan to a subprime borrower, and the borrower refuses to pay, the Left paints the borrower as the victim and the bank as the villain. To the Left, lenders are "banksters," not pillars of the community. The Left will most assuredly move to sever the legal obligation for massive numbers of citizens to pay their debts to politically unpopular lenders.

This is always the risk of bond investing, that the borrower will default and leave the lender holding the bag. Equity (stock) investors are in a different position. They get their fair share (as the word "equity" implies) of the profits. This form of investment puts the shareholders' interest in sync with the company's interest. They're in it together. The risks to equity investors are either poor management or a general economic downturn.

To really understand the difference between the two types of investment you need to forget for a moment the technical connotations of the words "equity" and "bond." Remember the older, moral meaning from which the financial meaning was derived. Equity is a just division of the profits of an enterprise. Bonds are promises, moral commitments, as in "his word is his bond." Equity investments are threatened by a general stagnation, which leaves the owners with little or no profit to divide among themselves. Bond investments, on the other hand, are threatened by a general environment dominated by political promise breakers, who set aside the traditional principle of the sanctity of contracts.

That's why the normal rules don't apply here. The old dictum that stocks are good in an expansion and bonds are good in a recession does not hold. It did not hold during the 1970s (a period with a policy mix much like the current one).

> An old wives tale says that the stock market is the optimistic market and the bond market is the pessimistic market. The stock market loves strong economic growth while the bond market hates it. Bonds are considered defensive investments, while stocks are considered offensive investments. The whole view, however, is highly suspect. Both the bond market and the stock market performed horribly in the 1970s, but they have both performed well in the 1980s and 1990s. Interest rates shot up during the stagflation in the 1970s, but they have trended down ever since. Despite the strong economic growth and rising stock markets of the New Era, bond yields have consistently come down and bond investors have experienced solid performance even though the economy has been strong.
>
> —BRIAN WESBURY, *The New Era of Wealth*

Stagflation is a stock and a bond killer at the same time. The stagnation kills stocks and the inflation kills bonds. The current judicial climate, despite some movement to the left, has tended to uphold contract rights, which are treated as sacrosanct in the actual text of the Constitution. But what if it shifts further left? And even if the courts continue to enforce the nominal value of politically unpopular contracts, they have no recognized authority to preserve the dollar in which those contracts are repaid. This leaves inflation, the oldest form of debt default, firmly in place. Bondholders during the Nixon/Ford/Carter years learned that lesson at the cost of large capital losses. I would rather you learn from their mistake than pay the same tuition yourself.

> The period between 1965 and 1982 was the worst 17-year period in the U.S. stock market history. After adjustment for inflation, investors in U.S. stocks during that period saw negative returns. This period should show investors that stocks do not always go up. Investors would have beaten both stocks and bonds during this period by investing in short-term money-market instruments.
>
> —BRIAN WESBURY, *The New Era of Wealth*

Let's say, however, that I'm wrong. That has happened before and will probably happen again. Let's say we don't get the inflation that I predict. Perhaps the credit markets stay frozen; banks continue to hoard cash; newly printed money stays locked in the vault and money in circulation falls. That happened to Japan in the 1990s. Even though the odds don't seem to favor it at the moment, it is a sufficiently plausible scenario, so we should already have a plan in place in case of a prolonged deflationary recession à la Japan.

If we get a Japanese scenario, bonds are still a highly risky investment, not because of inflation but because of deflation. Deflationary recessions tend to trigger large increases in bankruptcies. That's because revenues fall (due both to a lower volume of sales and lower prices for the small number of items that the business actually does manage to sell), but interest payments do not. Generally debt service payments are fixed annual amounts; they don't go up when times are good, or down when times are bad: they stay the same in good years and in bad. So, when revenues fall and interest payments don't, many companies with a lot of debt are forced to seek the protection of bankruptcy. Think of it this way: stocks bend, but bonds break. Once they break, bond investors find themselves in the bankruptcy court system, where the game is largely tilted against them. Bondholders' contracts are automatically dissolved and, except in the few cases where the bonds are guaranteed by assets (which, in this deflation scenario, are falling in value anyway) the investors have little power.

This raises the issue of niches in which to invest in bonds. We've mentioned some above: bonds issued by companies that are likely to be politically protected from bankruptcy are appealing for the high risk–high reward section of your portfolio. It may also be worthwhile for your Japanese deflationary recession playbook to contain a list of companies that have low enough levels of debt that they can survive a deflationary downturn. The bonds of companies that are unusually suited to survive a lengthy deflationary recession are like the baby that gets thrown out with the bathwater. Less insightful investors will tend to see all bonds as too high-risk. Deflation-resistant companies will tend to get undervalued in a generalized wave of anxiety about credit worthiness.

These companies are a good opportunity for you to get superior income gains should a Japanese-style deflation occur. In addition to relatively low debt loads, your target companies should also have flexible labor forces and no other long-term contracts that commit them to fixed expenses. Let me emphasize that this strategy will only work in a time of deflation. You generally don't want to be a bondholder in times of inflation.

However, there is an exception to this rule. There is a kind of bond that insures you against the risk of inflation. They are called Treasury Inflation-Protected Securities, TIPS for short. TIPS are issued by the federal government so there is virtually no risk of default, and the payment is recalculated regularly using a principal amount that rises and falls in the general price level according to the Consumer Price Index. In other words, the amount of money you lend to the government is theoretically increased by the amount of inflation, then the higher amount is used to calculate a higher interest payment for you. If you believe, as I and most free-market economists do, that the CPI tends to overstate the level of inflation, you should want TIPS even more. They pay you the politically exaggerated inflation rate rather than the actual lower one.

You will not get rich on TIPS. They're for the safe portion of your diversified portfolio. This isn't a gambling book and you're not in Las Vegas. Don't put it all at risk. You should have a supersafe section of your portfolio. You'll sleep better, and well-rested people make better decisions.

As you see, in this environment, if you're going to be a lender, you must be careful to be the right kind of lender: the kind who can hold the threat of bankruptcy over a politically favored industry, or the type who has some other form of protection against inflationary default or the type whom the Left needs in order to finance their pet projects. The next section is devoted to the third type of investor, the bondholders whom the Democratic coalition needs to keep things going.

## The Municipal Bond Complex

Liberals like to build things: roads and bridges, yes, but most of all liberals like to build schools. When a left-of-center presidential candidate says something like "we must rebuild our infrastructure," he means "we must pour enormous amounts of money into public schools." What he wants you to hear is "we must get rid of these potholes and create another highway into town so that you can shave ten minutes off your commute," when actually he wants to pay off one of his central political constituencies with your money, and make it seem as though he's doing something for you.

You are an investor and therefore you cannot afford any political illusions: the Obama economy is dominated by public works projects, but unlike the New Deal, the money is being focused away from the kind of genuinely public infrastructure projects like dams and bridges, which we all use, and more precisely targeted at special-interest constituencies like public education, public transit, and subsidized energy sectors. For a Saul Alinsky–trained community organizer, all policy is about the acquisition and retention of power.

The Left, unlike the Right, is more of a consortium than a coalition. It's a giant business that depends for its profits on political power. Pro-lifers don't make money on an abortion avoided; in fact, they'll probably find themselves offering aid to the mother. Many pro-abortion people, on the other hand, do make money on the abortions. School choice people, generally, don't make money on school vouchers; the voucher programs are very small pilot programs with few participants allowed, and the vouchers themselves don't always cover the cost of education. In addition, the schools are nonprofits with very low wage scales. Nobody gets rich on vouchers, but plenty of people are making enormous sums of money from the public educational system.

The Left makes money on its causes. The union movement is dominated by public sector unions, and the public sector unions get all of their money from the taxes that the rest of us pay. The mortgage finance system is dominated by government-sponsored entities like Fannie Mae and Freddie Mac. Between them, they share 80 percent of the mortgages that pass through the system and out into the investment markets. They fund the American Left with the money they get from huge government subsidies. But home builders have to actually earn their money.

My point here is not to get you to think "Left: bad; Right: good." My point is to help you to understand how the world works, so you can make money in any environment.

HERE'S HOW THE world of infrastructure spending is going to work:

Almost everything big is built with borrowed money. State and local governments borrow their money by selling bonds to investors. To help encourage this process, the federal government allows the investors to exclude their interest income from these bonds from their taxable income. Not surprisingly, these investments are called municipal bonds, or "munis." There's quite a large volume of them out there already, but we're going to get a lot more over the next several years. That's because nearly every stage of the municipal bonds complex is a source of income for politically connected interest groups.

My education in the world of government finance began in 1995. I was the president of the first free market think tank in America focused on local policy issues. I, personally, had helped elect the first Republican majority in Pittsburgh's Allegheny County in over seventy years. They had pledged an ambitious agenda of tax cuts and privatization, and they were elected on that basis. But they had no idea how to implement it. For this, they turned to me.

When I first began to spend time in the marbled hallways of political power, I expected the conversations to be about policy. I was wrong. Everywhere I turned I found conversations about vendors. "Who would get this contract or that one?" Not: "What would we privatize or deregulate?"

As the newspapers began to write more and more about my role as an advisor, I found myself with many new friends, and even more lunch invitations. Most of my new friends worked for firms with the word "capital" in the title. When I asked them what they did for a living, they said "investment banking." I had met investment bankers before, but those were private sector guys. They didn't wine and dine mayors and county commissioners. The regular kind of investment bankers' offices weren't near city hall. But the kind of investment bankers I was meeting in 1995 could generally walk to city hall in less than a minute.

My next set of new friends was better at talking, but not as good at math. They were lawyers. Their tasseled shoes also saw little wear in a walk to the mayor's office. They were distantly attached to the XYZ Capital guys. They would show up at the same fund-raising events and cluster together in friendly huddles. That's when I first learned that there was a job called "bond counsel." Apparently every time government borrows money in the bond market, a lawyer has to write up the documents and attest that these bonds genuinely qualify as tax-free municipals. There's a lawyer for the government, and a separate lawyer for the bank that issues the bonds. It turns out that often there's more than one law firm on each bond. The second one is called co-counsel. And there is often more than one investment bank involved. The second one is called "co-underwriter." The first banks and the first law firms don't like this, but the politicians sometimes make them do it. And all of the lawyers and all of the bankers have given money to the Committee to Elect So-and-So, or the So-and-So Good Government Committee.

Well, it used to be that way, but eventually things got so out of hand that the bankers were told they weren't allowed to give any more money to the politicians. So after that, I saw that lots of checks were coming in from Mrs. Investment Banker, although it was still Mr. Investment Banker who showed up at the annual fund-raiser for the Committee to Reelect So-and-So. Nice, how the wives took an interest in politics.

My third group of friends was very good at math, and very bad at choosing ties. They were engineers. They designed and built all of the stuff that was designed and built with municipal bond money. They were infrastructure guys. The first time I was invited to speak at the Engineers Society of Pittsburgh, I was a little surprised. I'd never taken a course in engineering, and had done only marginally well in physics. I didn't meet any chemical engineers that day, or anyone who designed computer chips for automobiles. But sewage guys, we had a flood of them. I had been involved in a plan to privatize the sewage system, and a private operator would not have the same set of friends as the water and sewer authority. Even worse, he might not have any friends at all. He might actually hire consulting engineers in a competitive bidding process. That's why the Engineers Society invited me to a luncheon/panel discussion on the pros and cons of privatization. I was the only pro against several cons, including the moderator. I didn't eat the lunch; the whole thing made me kind of sick.

That's the day I learned that the debate of sewer privatization was much more about the sewage that ran through city hall than the sewage that ran under it. It was about political patronage.

My third group of new friends didn't even pretend to be anything other than what they were: public unions. They build the stuff, run it, and fix it. The more stuff that's built, the more jobs for this army of friends of ward leaders and brothers-in-law of Democratic committee members. They wanted their stadia/convention centers/water and sewer treatment plants/bus-ways to nowhere to be built, and built by the politicians that they helped to elect and financed by the bond guys who procured the money. If you didn't go along with that, they shoved you around or slashed your tires.

So, America, here's your new infrastructure team: politically connected bond counsels, underwriters, consulting engineers and architects and union bosses who control the guys who build it all and run it. They are the reasons that political campaigns have so very much money to spend on advertising. They're the reason that public debt expands in good times and in bad. They're the reason that the little guy has almost no chance of influencing policy. And they're the guys you're going to use to survive this present anti-wealth business climate—because you are going to become a municipal bond investor.

Municipal bonds are key to getting you through the next several years. Munis are securities offered by local governments to the general public in order to borrow money to finance spending in excess of revenues. In short, a muni is an IOU from city hall to you, plus interest. What makes them so very important just now is that the interest you're going to receive from these bonds will, generally, be tax-free. That's why quite a few people who never gave much serious thought to this particular investment in a controlled tax environment will need to give it serious thought in a rising tax environment. Since munis offer the privilege of tax-free income, they pay a lower rate of interest. If I can get 4 percent interest on a Federal Treasury bond, and 4 percent interest on a state municipal bond, then which will I choose? I'll choose the muni because the interest is not taxed. But, of course, I'm not the only one who will make that choice. Investors who pay attention to tax liability gravitate toward munis and the sellers of those investments know that, so they can sell munis for lower interest rates than taxable-income bonds. You're willing to take maybe 3 percent on a muni tax-free instead of 4 percent on a comparable bond that is taxable, because what matters to you is your after-tax income. Remember your first paycheck? It didn't matter what your gross pay was, the number on the stub of the paycheck; you cared about your take-home pay. Well, bond investors are the same way. There is a formula you can use to calculate the comparable level of income between a muni and a taxable bond. It goes like this:

What precise corporate bond yield would the investor need to equal the tax-exempt return to the muni being considered? To answer this question, you must convert the tax-free yield into the equivalent taxable yield. The formula is:

$$\text{Taxable equivalent yield} = \frac{\textit{Tax-free yield (\%)}}{\textit{100\% - Tax bracket (\%)}} \underline{\qquad\qquad\qquad}$$

For example, an investor is in the 28% tax bracket. She purchases a municipal bond paying a tax-free rate of 6%. She is also considering a corporate bond with a yield of 7.5%. Which bond—the muni or the corporate—offers her the greatest yield after taxes?

$$\text{Taxable equivalent yield} = \frac{\textit{Tax-free yield (\%)}}{\textit{100\% - Tax bracket (\%)}} \underline{\qquad\qquad\qquad}$$

$$= \frac{6\%}{100\% - 28\%} \underline{\qquad\qquad\qquad}$$

$$= 8.33\%$$

To get the same after-tax yield as the muni, the corporate bonds have to offer an 8.33% return. The investor buys the muni.

—ROBERT ZIPF, *How the Bond Market Works*

Don't let the math worry you. You should have your broker or advisor actually run the calculation for you. I put the formula there for the purpose of illustrating the principle. You see that a 6 percent tax-free yield is equivalent to an 8.33 percent taxable yield if you are in the 28 percent tax bracket. Your take-home pay is the same with a muni that pays 6 percent as it is with a Treasury bond that pays 8.33 percent.

But what if your tax rate goes up? What if your tax rate were to rise from 28 percent to, say, 50 percent? Then you would need a 12 percent interest rate to keep pace with a 6 percent nontaxable bond. As you can see, the higher the tax rate, the more valuable tax-free income becomes. In times of high taxes, munis are highly prized, and this drives up their value.

If you think taxes are going to rise under Obama, you should look closely at municipal bonds as an investment. If you think taxes are going to fall under Obama, then you should stay away from them. You will probably not be surprised to learn that municipal bond values tended generally to rise and fall with the probability of an Obama election during the campaign season. The correlation is not perfect, because the credit crisis had an unexpected impact on municipal bond insurers that created some temporary distortions. However, by and large as investors felt more threatened by an Obama victory, they sought solace in the arms of the muni bond salesman.

If this is the case, you ask, isn't the tax advantage of a municipal bond already reflected in their price? The answer is "yes, partly." The current pricing of municipal bonds reflects a degree of uncertainty about future tax hikes. As of this writing, bond investors are betting that Obama will not be a big tax hiker. And as of this writing, despite all evidence to the contrary, the market is reflecting a consensus (or a hope) that Obama is very much like Bill Clinton and will impose only modest tax increases. I think otherwise, for the reasons given above. I think that Obama's economic philosophy did not shift as he made the transition from community organizer to state senator, or as he made the transition from state senator to U.S. senator, nor from senator to presidential candidate. I do not believe that a presidential election changed his core worldview, nor does a midterm congressional election. He thinks that high taxes on upper-income earners are essential to fund a massive spending program that is essential to "heal" the economy.

Given the intellectual framework of his economics, why would he not raise taxes? Why would he not raise taxes at least as much as he promised to do even before the current severe economic crisis gave him warrant to raise them even more?

There are a number of different types of municipal bonds distinguished variously by public versus private use; taxable preference; time span of repayment; source of revenues and risk of default. Even if you make the right decision about whether to go muni, you still are left with the decision about what kind of muni to buy.

The time span of the bonds should correspond as closely as possible with the expected time span of the expected tax hikes. In other words, if you think taxes are going to be high for the next five years, buy five-year munis. If you think taxes are going to be high for the next ten years, buy ten-year munis. If you think taxes are going to be high for the next thirty years, move to Estonia and start over.

You may not be able to get exactly what you want. Small and medium-sized investors tend for many reasons to buy municipal bonds indirectly through mutual funds or exchange-traded funds (ETFs). This means you are, to some degree, at the mercy of the company that assembles the portfolio in question. As of this writing, Vanguard has a muni ETF that contains a range of bonds whose average term is roughly seven years. No, it's not a perfect two-Obama-term fit, but it's pretty close. As you see, you want to adjust accordingly. This is very much easier if you are a large and sophisticated investor, because you are in a position to purchase individual municipal bonds at reasonably favorable terms.

If you have that kind of flexibility, then you can tailor your strategy even more precisely. Look for general obligation bonds instead of revenue bonds. The former are as good as the full faith and credit of the unit of government that issues them; the latter are usually secured by some specific revenue stream. For example, airport revenue bonds pay their interest from the revenues they get from ticket surcharges, landing fees, concession fees, and so on. Turnpike authorities use tolls. Revenue bonds are not immune to an economic downturn; if people stop flying, you don't want to own airport revenue bonds.

There's another reason to tread cautiously when dealing with revenue bonds. They often are tied to projects that are not as effective at tax minimization as is generally the case. When bonds are used to support projects deemed to be for private use, such as stadiums and hospitals, they are imbued with a weaker form of tax exemption. The tax code has a feature that forces you to add the interest income back to your return as something called a "preference." If you have enough preferences, you're forced to pay the Alternative Minimum Tax (AMT). This is complicated stuff. I had trouble doing this calculation back when I actually was a tax accountant, and I seriously doubt that I could do it now. In addition, AMT rules are in a constant state of political flux, so no general-purpose investment book could really be relied on as the final word on how to deal with AMT issues. Use a pro. Don't use Tim Geithner, even if he promises to use TurboTax.

General obligation bonds, on the other hand, are, well, a general obligation of the city, county, or state that issues them. They have to be paid unless the government goes bankrupt. Governments almost never go bankrupt. Even Republicans hardly ever let a government go bankrupt, and the Left certainly would not let any major American city do so. The Obama administration has already supported massive transfer payments to state and local governments just for the purpose of stimulus. I seriously doubt that a political culture that did not let banks and automakers fail would leave all those unionized local government employees without their bailout should the time come.

But if you think I'm wrong, and muni bond prices as of this writing show that many investors do, then restrict your purchases to the roughly one-half of the market that is insured against loss. Your rewards won't be as high, since those securities are not selling at the same depressed prices, but if you feel like you need to wear both a belt and suspenders at the same time, who am I to judge?

## Inflated Expectations

You would not be fully prepared to deal with the investment challenges ahead if you were not informed regarding the risk factors associated with high inflation. This factor is pervasive to the whole economy, and to the entire dollar-denominated financial system, not just the debt investment markets but debt investments are particularly directly vulnerable to inflation. That is because a bond is a promise in which the issuer of the bond is legally bound to pay you a fixed number of dollars at regular intervals until the final principal amount is repaid. Bonds are promises of future dollars. But if future dollars decline in value, the promise will turn out to have been worth less than if the dollars had held their value.

There are other risk factors associated with bonds, such as the risk of default. But with high-quality bonds the risk of default is very low, so the risk of inflation tends to drive the changes in value of most of the bond market.

Here is how it works: If an investor believes that a bond is more risky than it previously had been, then he will insist on a higher rate of return to compensate him for that risk.

For example, suppose you were willing to lend money to the U.S. government for five years at a 3 percent yield when you expected no inflation. What would you do if you came to believe that the price level would increase at 2 percent per year over the next five years? You would be unwilling to lend at a 3 percent rate any longer. You would insist on something much closer to a 5 percent yield to compensate for that loss of value. If you got a 5 percent rate in a 2 percent inflation environment, that would put you back in the same place as you would have been under our first supposition, with a real (that is, inflation-adjusted) return of 3 percent. The borrower would have paid you more dollars to compensate you for the fact that each dollar is worth less.

Things get a little more complicated when you move away from U.S. government–issued bonds toward riskier ones. The default risk increases. U.S. Treasury bonds are generally treated for theoretical purposes as though they pose no default risk. That has never been true, but it is becoming even less true by the day. So the difference between Treasury bonds and high-quality corporate bonds is not really the difference between riskless and more risky bonds: it is really the difference between two levels of default risk. To make matters more complicated, the distinction between default risk and inflation risk is not as rational as it is generally presented. After all, in the case of government debt, that same government controls the money supply, and by extension, the rate of inflation. Such governments can deliberately inflate away most of their debt liability by simply debasing the currency. In such a case inflation is not something different from default: inflation is the means of default.

Our levels of spending and indebtedness, combined with structural increases in spending in the form of middle-class entitlements, such as universal health care, make default seem more likely than at any time in our modern history. Will we default directly, or will we default through debasement? It seems the latter is the more likely. After all, the governing philosophy of the executive branch, the legislative branch, and the central bank has been overwhelmingly influenced by Keynesianism, the view that currency debasement is the preferred tool to stimulate growth through consumer spending. In addition, trade unions, who seem to have the ear of this administration, if not lower-elevation body parts, favor a debased currency as a tool of trade policy. They, and the large corporations they work for, believe that a less valuable dollar helps to protect them from foreign competition. So that constitutes another constituency for inflation.

In short, inflation is coming, and inflation is generally bad for bonds.

Are there any ways to make money in bonds in an inflationary environment? Yes, there are, but they are off the beaten paths of finance.

The general principle is to avoid bonds that promise to pay you a fixed number of dollars in favor of bonds that promise to pay you something else. For example, Treasury Inflation-Protected Securities (TIPS) promise to pay you a number of dollars that varies with the rate of inflation. At the end of the bond period, instead of getting back the amount you lent the government, you get back that amount plus an additional bonus to compensate you for the loss of dollar value. TIPS are a little complicated, so, as with everything else in this book, you're going to need a good advisor to work out the financial details and tax consequences, but TIPS are a great place to begin looking for inflation protection.

Some bonds promise to pay you fixed numbers of something other than dollars. For example, there are commodity-backed bonds. They have an element that is triggered under certain conditions, and pay you a commodity rather than a currency. These are very complicated instruments.

A more practical alternative is to look at bonds denominated in currencies other than dollars. The United States is not the only government that sells bonds to the public and U.S. companies are not the only companies that do the same. If you are looking for bond yields, but without the risks associated with the loss of dollar value, then foreign bonds are very attractive alternatives. Some government bonds are of similarly very low outright default risk as U.S. Treasuries. In those cases, you would be betting that the currency in which those bonds are denominated will be stronger than the dollar. As the United States drifts away from our fundamental principles of free market economics and sound currency, a number of nations drift toward them. As this unfolds gradually, global markets may be slow to see the ways in which the United States is losing stability relative to the rest of the world. This will likely cause "spreads"—that is, differences in yield between U.S. bonds and foreign bonds, which are based on the old habit of thinking of the United States as the safest haven. Over time, those spreads are likely to close if the United States continues its drift. People who saw the danger in U.S. bonds and the opportunity in foreign ones before the rest of the world will be rewarded with higher returns.

# CHAPTER SEVEN

# Equity Investment Strategies

## How to Surf the Green Recession

The bad news is that state interventions into free markets are by and large harmful to the public good. The good news is that these interventions cause harm in predictable patterns. (The science of political economy is the discipline that studies those patterns.)

For example, price floors cause gluts. If the market rate for lifeguards is $6 per hour, and the state makes it illegal for teenagers to sell their lifeguard services for less than $7 per hour, then there will be a glut of teenagers looking for lifeguard jobs. We saw this in the sudden spike in teenage unemployment in 2008 on the heels of a nationwide minimum-wage hike. The government can stop employers from hiring lifeguards for less than $7 per hour, but that is not the same thing as forcing them to hire lifeguards for $7 per hour or more. The employers have another option: fewer lifeguards. When you forbid sellers to offer goods and services for less than some arbitrary floor that falls below the rate at which they would voluntarily be willing to sell, then you cause a glut, an overabundance of the resource being sold. When we are free, the price drops to an amount to which the buyer and seller both agree, but when we are not free, the transaction does not occur.

Supply disruptions work in similar ways: they raise the price of goods above the natural level and discourage their consumption. Supply disruptions cause shortages. It is important that you understand this basic principle at this moment in history, because our national energy policy amounts to a series of planned supply disruptions. What wars and earthquakes and tsunamis did to us in the past, disrupting our ability to take fuel from the ground, we now do to ourselves through government fiat.

This is done in a number of ways.

First, there are prohibitions both official and unofficial against drilling for oil and natural gas. It is still illegal to drill for oil in most of the outer continental shelf and on vast swaths of domestic federally controlled property. Even in those few places where it is nominally legal, the permitting process strongly favors environmental activists, who are able to gum up the system with nuisance complaints. Even under the pro-drilling Bush administration this caused tremendous delays. Imagine what the anti-drilling Obama administration would do with this byzantine process. The Department of the Interior has enormous discretion when it comes to issuing drilling permits. It has enormous discretion when it comes to delays in the process. It can decide which objections are legitimate, requiring detailed examination and rebuttal, and which are frivolous. In the short period of time leading up to the Bush administration's decision to rescind the Carter executive order that banned offshore drilling, the number of permit objections filed spiked by an amazing 700 percent over previous numbers. Foundation-funded anti-oil groups can simply clog the system with frivolous objections.

Under Bush, many of those would likely have been thrown out as transparently ideological objections to drilling. Under Obama, we can expect endless delays, which will make it impossible for oil companies to ever put drill to earth. Of course, Congress will complain that the oil companies are not drilling the acreage that is already approved for drilling. One in a thousand citizens is aware of the abuse of the permitting process by the Left both within and without the government.

All of this adds up to much higher energy prices. That is not an unintended consequence of the intervention; it is a very much intended consequence. The point is to discourage consumption of fossil fuels. The point is to make it expensive to drive or fly. The Left has decided that carbon, the chemical basis of all organic life on earth, is a pollutant. Remember that during the campaign the president was quoted as saying that although he objected to the pace of increase, he supported the goal of making gasoline more expensive.

During the campaign candidate Obama sat down for an interview with my CNBC colleague, John Harwood.

HARWOOD: As difficult as this is for consumers right now, is, in fact, high gas prices what we need to let the market work, a line incentive so that we do shift to alternative means of energy?

SEN. OBAMA: Well, I think that we have been slow to move in a better direction when it comes to energy usage. And the president, frankly, hasn't had an energy policy. And as a consequence, we've been consuming energy as if it's infinite. We now know that our demand is badly outstripping supply with China and India growing as rapidly as they are. So . . .

HARWOOD: So could these high prices help us?

SEN. OBAMA: I think that I would have preferred a gradual
  adjustment. The fact that this is such a shock to American
  pocketbooks is not a good thing. But if we take some steps
  right now to help people make the adjustment, first of all
  by putting more money into their pockets, but also by encouraging the market to adapt to these new circumstances
  more quickly, particularly U.S. automakers, then I think
  ultimately we can come out of this stronger and have a
  more efficient energy policy than we do right now.

Every five-year plan that phases out one form of energy has
to include an element that encourages others. Lenin, for example, hated wood and steam, but was obsessed with electricity.
He imbued electricity with virtually mystical powers to bring
about a utopia on earth. Every one of his Five-Year Plans included highly compulsory mandates for electricity production.
The main problem (among many) is that Lenin had already
nationalized the "commanding heights" of industry, including
coal production. Inefficient coal meant inefficient energy, and
the electricity-obsessed Soviets lagged behind the let-consumers-
decide Americans in the spread of electrification.

Now it is "renewable" energy that is imbued with mystical
powers. It promises to end sprawl, renew the rust belt, catapult
America to global economic dominance, end terrorism, and,
of course, save us all from the fiery torments of the greenhouse
effect. The president has pledged a doubling of renewable
energy production over the next three years. This is a very ambitious goal and would require some kind of genetic splice of
a Manhattan Project and a Marshall Plan to accomplish. Even
if it can be achieved, since renewables are roughly 5 percent of

production now, a doubling of their share would still leave us depending on the nonrenewables for 90 percent of our energy. So we'd still be overwhelmingly dependent on carbon-based energy, despite government policies that would make carbon more expensive.

This policy is a prescription for at least two disasters about which investors should be aware.

First, it will create an enormously expensive honey pot that further corrupts our political class. This honey pot is not your opportunity; it is your temptation.

Alternative energy will sit atop the whole mess as the official corporate welfare queen. But none of the money is for public shareholders. The political class will go to great pains to make sure that the money doesn't go to "Wall Street." The money must go to the unionized workers and the politically favored nonprofit advocacy groups that help elect members of Congress.

Some investors will make money, but not you. Private equity players, such as hedge funds and venture capital, will do especially well in alternative energy. But these rewards go overwhelmingly to those firms that are politically well connected. They'll know which bill is passing which key committee and when. They'll know where the strings are attached and which firms can maneuver through those strings. They'll know exactly when to invest and with whom. They'll have more lobbyists than engineers on the payroll. They know more about the political process than you do. And, make no mistake, this is a political process.

Warren Buffett once said that if you sit down to play poker and within twenty minutes you don't know who the patsy is, then you're the patsy. Let me save you the twenty minutes and the lost stake. In the game of public subsidy, you are the patsy.

Honest nonpolitical shareholders are the patsy. Don't buy alternative energy stocks; it's too difficult to determine which one will perform because they do so based on preferential government treatment and contracts.

Second, high energy prices place a drag on the entire American economy. The more energy-dependent the industry, the more vulnerable it is to energy shocks. This is your investment opportunity.

For instance, energy consumers are hurt by anti-production energy policies. The normal course of economic history is that commodities prices fall over time. This is as true for energy as it is for other commodities. Energy is the "master commodity," though: that is, energy is the commodity that we use to turn all of the other commodities into useful products. This means that energy is a pervasive commodity. It shows up in everything. Its price fluctuations affect all others.

There is no substitute for energy. If there is a global copper shortage, you can often switch to steel (hence the coin collector's "white penny"). Foods are even more interchangeable in response to price fluctuations. Patties made from ground beef give way to ground turkey, then ground chicken, and finally ground pork.

Though there is some substitution effect between energy commodities, it is much more difficult. We use oil to make gasoline. We could switch to ethanol, but that requires different kinds of engines, and even more important, a completely alien production process.

We use coal to generate most of our electricity. Yes, we can also use natural gas, but again, the production process is different. Technically you can run autos on natural gas, too, but the changes are even more dramatic than the changes needed to use ethanol.

It is common for the alternative energy lobby to emphasize the ways in which scientists have solved these problems,
but science was never the problem. The problems have always
been economic. Ethanol isn't the new fuel; it's the old fuel.
Before Henry Ford launched the commercial auto business,
most cars and tractors ran on ethanol. Ford decided to go with
the newer fuel, petroleum, and thus it has been ever since. The
same applies to windmills. Wind is a late medieval technology, as is water. Don Quixote tilted at windmills before the
Renaissance. The problem is reliability and control. As Jesus
of Nazareth once said, "The wind bloweth whithersoever it
will." The implications are as economic as they are theologi-
cal. A production process that depends on interruptible natural
processes is inconsistent with a modern economy. So is one that
frequently can be found far away from the places where most
end users live.

The long and short of all of this is the fact that alternative energy sources are not remotely plausible short-term or
midterm sources of energy in the quantities needed to run the
world. Not now, not for a very, very long time. It took us a
century to build our current parallel energy grids (coal, electricity generation, transmission, and distribution, on the one
hand, and oil well, refinery, shipping, and retail distribution
on the other hand). And most of that development occurred
in an environment of low population density and permissive
land-use laws. A complete reboot from carbon to hydrogen or
the capricious gifts of nature, such as sunshine, wind, and rain,
in and around a world of NIMBYs with lawyers is probably the
most difficult endeavor any society has ever attempted. Forget
the Manhattan Project analogy: think Manhattan Project on
a Rubik's Cube while being sued by an angry divorce lawyer.

So, while we chase waterfalls and strangle the only practical energy system we have, expect an era of high energy prices. This creates a veritable army of victims: commuters, airlines, truckers, couriers, and any industry that depends on shipping. Think about farmers and manufacturers in a new world where shipping becomes the chief cost of production. Think of weight as the new proxy for cost. The heavier, the harder to ship. Steel, coal, water, and so on become a cost center that, literally, weighs down income statements of every vendor in the supply management chain. We've gotten used to a world of global sourcing—that is, bringing stuff together from far-flung places in the world to be combined into durable goods in farther-flung places in the world before they are all shipped back here to America. Forget all of that. Even if we manage to escape the political backlash against global trade, high energy prices impose a kind of de facto protectionism on anything that weighs much.

If you can think of a way to help the world deal with these problems, the world is your oyster (but I recommend that you ship it without those heavy shells).

Supply management has to be redone with much shorter lines. Computers will be used to run the algorithms. Someone needs to write the new software and keep it updated. That software needs to be updated with minute-by-minute spot checks for energy prices, and with the best available energy cost forecasts. Yes, a lot of that is being done already, but it gets much more important from now on. The skill sets are as dispersed as the supply chain. The kind of guy who knows how to write that software is not the same kind of guy as the one who knows how to figure out energy prices, and neither of those guys are the type to be especially good at geography. If you are one of the above three types, find the two others and you've got a business in the world of high energy prices.

Most of the energy consumption grid is just plain dumb. Water and sewer plants run all the time, generally, instead of powering up and down with times of high and low prices. The electricity grid has very little intelligence imbedded in it. It just runs around the clock and you dip into the stream of electrons when you need them. This always could have been done much more efficiently, but because we've always used cheap coal to run cheap turbines that push cheap electrons through the wire, we've never needed to be efficient before now. Now we all need to be efficient. This is good for the chip manufacturers. Although chip manufacturing is not much of a small-business kind of opportunity, installing them is. So is programming them. Ditto for industrial training. Someone needs to teach Nick down at the sewage plant how to run the newfangled thing.

There is a great deal of room in the economy, I think, for a kind of one-plus electrician and one-minus engineer, a guy who knows more than Mr. Buttcrack but less than Mr. Pocket Protector. What one engineer designs, ten thousand technicians install. Not good with your hands? Maybe you are good with people, and if you are good with the kind of people who are good with their hands, then you've got a business. Get them trained, educated—yes, but apprenticed, too. Learn how to manage guys who wouldn't be caught dead in a cubicle. If a generation of Americans all want to wear ties, then find pockets of hungry and reliable immigrants. Bond with them and their leaders; get to know their priest; earn their trust.

The lost art of geography will need a revival, most of all the lost art of local geography. In a world of high gas prices, Mr. Shortcut is the king of the world. Some smart shipping entrepreneur is going to get beyond the "traffic and weather on the eights" level and begin to integrate the cheap revolution in GPS with satellite imaging and traffic management. FedEx is experimenting with a local franchise model. You don't work for FedEx, you own your local route. Finding the shortest route isn't just a matter of knowing the best shortcuts; it's a matter of knowing when they are best and worst, and not just normally, but today. Shaving a tenth of the cost off of a delivery is a profit booster when it's a package from Amazon, but when you're driving a double-wide loaded with steel, it's the difference between poverty and prosperity.

Farming is about to be transformed. The average food item is shipped twelve hundred miles to your door. Forget the guilt about the social and environmental impact; I have. That long trip is fine with me. I don't believe that strawberries have human rights and certainly not the right to avoid an unplanned long trip. I don't care about the carbon footprint, which is minuscule. I have no ideological commitment to local growing. In fact, I have a slight ideological commitment against it. I want to have a bunch of farmers in South America tied to my prosperity. I want them to not want anyone to blow me up, because they want me to keep buying their strawberries. My zeal for more local farming isn't an environmental kind of green; it's the financial kind. In an anti-energy environment, fortunes will be made in shaving a few hundred miles off that twelve hundred. Regional farms are well positioned to do that.

Are there ways to help translate giant agribusiness efficiency practices into a regional farm situation? If so, use them to farm. Or, if Green Acres is not the life for you, consult with someone else on how to do it. Are there ways to use local foodstuffs as substitutes for global ingredients? Experiment in your kitchen. Maybe it's a restaurant opportunity, or a new food product that can be sold in stores, or a cookbook or a cooking show. Look at the ingredients that are rising in price rapidly because of energy policy and see if there is a cheaper local alternative and start experimenting.

## Media Suppression Workarounds

Media fortunes have always been created in that world of overlap between regulation and freedom. The great broadcast media conglomerates were formed by men who understood the regulatory environment and adapted themselves to it. Yes, Marconi solved the technical problems, but the fortunes were made by guys who saw the implications of government-granted spectrum monopolies before anyone else. Heritage broadcast stations—that is, stations that were granted the first licenses— dominated the media landscape for decades until the next child of regulation appeared: cable. Local governments grant franchises to a cable operator, and that makes them the monopoly. Theoretically they could offer more than one franchise, and a very small number of municipalities do, but for all practical purposes local cable operators are monopolies. The Internet has been much less regulated, and from a content standpoint is basically impervious to regulation. Still, the libertarian electrons and photons have to pass through highly regulated cables and wires, so the new regulatory regime will change the economics of Internet media even though it cannot police the content.

Under the new left regulatory regime we will likely see a number of changes that will determine what the future of media is.

First, there are the changes that regulatory Republicans already had in the works. The change to high-definition TV will affect more than what kind of antenna you have to hook up to the back of your set. Part of the transition includes the creation of alternate channels. Most stations are looking at one main broadcast station and three other affiliated stations. For the most part those media companies that have already made the switch have little or no content to offer on their alternative channels. So the alternate channels are filled with reruns or, more likely, are altogether dark. The same thing is happening with FM radio. There will be one main digital station with very high fidelity that will be appropriate for music, and two affiliated channels with lower fidelity appropriate for voice.

Imagine a giant bellows in reverse. As these radio and TV stations under government mandate are forced to open, simultaneously, two or three new channels for every existing channel, they will create a vacuum. The market power will shift from content distributors to content providers. The bellows will open rapidly and suck all of the oxygen into itself at once. This is the opportunity for Ma and Pa to get into the media business.

Again, I don't want you to romanticize this. It is a huge cost burden to the media industry. Revenue streams are already at low flow, and now they'll be diverted into thousands of little tributaries. Many companies will go bankrupt; many more are so starved for working capital that they are unable to afford high-quality programming. Amateurs will foist their junk onto our screens via government diktat. Content will degrade from *High School Musical* to high school musicals. Most TV will just plain stink compared to what we have now, and if you think that TV already stinks—well, welcome to TV purgatory.

But the thing about the doctrine of purgatory is that it holds that improvement is possible. The suffering is redemptive. The souls trapped there can learn. They will need to learn two things: how to provide good content at low costs of production, and how to monetize the audience that they attract. The clever entrepreneurs who solve those two are the dominant players in the new highly regulated media.

Second, there is the "fairness" lobby. Brian Anderson and Adam Thierer have written a book titled *A Manifesto for Media Freedom*, in which they make a very persuasive case that America is moving into a period of unprecedented regulation of political speech.

> The "fairness" campaign was kicked off in 2004, when Media Matters for America, a newly formed liberal watchdog linked to George Soros, started an online campaign to encourage Congress to bring BACK THE FAIRNESS Doctrine.
>
> —BRIAN ANDERSON AND ADAM THIERER,
> *A Manifesto for Media Freedom*

Soros found himself a man who knew how to hit conservatives because he had worked for one of their flagship publications, the *American Spectator*. David Brock had done well for himself as an attack journalist for the right, but had undergone a dramatic public turnaround and became an attack journalist for the Left.

> "Tired of imbalanced political discourse on our airwaves?" asked David Brock, the head of Media Matters (and an apostate from conservatism). "By restoring a diversity of fact and opinion to programming, Fairness Doctrine legislation restores a concept that has been lost since the 1980s—that because the public is entitled to be adequately informed by the broadcasters of news and opinion."

The campaign gained little traction at a time when Democrats controlled neither House nor Senate. Yet given that Media Matters had connections not only with

SOROS "AFFILIATES" like MoveOn.org and the New Democrat Network, but also with the Clintons—John Podesta, formerly Bill Clinton's chief of staff, helped Brock get the group started—its early efforts merited more notice than they received.

—BRIAN ANDERSON AND ADAM THIERER,
*A Manifesto for Media Freedom*

Podesta, of course, as of this writing, is looking like a key figure in the Obama administration. The policy shop he ran, the Center for American Progress, was funded largely by Soros, and is already playing a role as a major policy shop for the Obama administration. It is unlikely that the administration would back away entirely from attempts to muzzle conservative media given the personnel decisions so far.

Of course, much has been made of the renewed threats to reimpose the infamous "fairness doctrine" on talk radio and other opinion outlets. Under the fairness doctrine, however, the threat is as effective as the reality. Seldom have stations been fined or shut down for failing to conform with the arbitrary content ratios of the federal regulators. The license granted by the FCC is far and away the most valuable asset the station possesses; even the most potent brand the station holds is virtually worthless without a slice of spectrum on which to broadcast. Even when it was in force, the doctrine, like most dictators, ruled more by intimidation than by execution.

I think that the fairness doctrine per se will ultimately fail to garner enough votes in Congress. It will be politically unpopular and will unite strands across the political spectrum in opposition. Yes, talk radio and Fox News have become almost Goldsteinian (see *1984*, by George Orwell) devil figures, but in the end, shutting down his opponents would confirm the

harshest Obama critics' contention that he is more like a Third
World strongman than like a traditional American president.

And besides, why put up with the backlash when you can
accomplish the same things with less effort? Broadcast outlets
are already licensed by the federal government. They already
have mandates in place requiring them to serve their commu-
nities. They already have a "public file" into which they place
documentary proof that they are serving the needs of the community. TV and radio both have these requirements. If you're
awake early this Sunday morning, pick up your remote and
click your way through your local broadcast stations. You'll
probably see two or three programs whose names are made
up of some combination of words like "community," "focus,"
"perspectives," and "region." The host is more than randomly
likely to be an African-American woman. This show is on the
air for one purpose—the public file. It's not there to get view-
ers. It's not there to please sponsors. It's not there because the
management has a burning desire to see more programming
about the problems of managing public housing, or cutbacks in
bus schedules. It's there so that the station doesn't get seized by
regulators and given to somebody else.

Obama has proposed that the Federal Communications
Commission ramp up these rules. Instead of license renewal
hearings happening every seven years, as is current policy, he
wants them held every two years. Instead of a public file and
self-disclosure, he wants a mandatory community board to
evaluate their content. Who do you think will show up for
those boards? The usual suspects. Radio stations already have
something called "ascertainment day," at which hosts and producers (usually the latter) sit through long presentations during
which they are harangued for not paying adequate attention to
issues of concern to racial minorities, women, the homeless,

addicts, the handicapped, and any other special-interest group that gets wind of the forum. The stations already do this voluntarily. President Obama will want it to be imposed on them.

None of this is fair. These stations spent untold millions of dollars to purchase their signals and develop an audience for them. They invested that way because the policy environment was one that encouraged wide freedom of expression. To change the rules on them in a stunning act of political retribution would constitute a terrible abuse of power. It would constitute something like a nationalization of the airwaves. Program quality would suffer. General managers would tell program directors to keep the content safe. Unable to hire an army of lawyers and monitors to play defense against well-funded community organizers, small radio stations would switch to music, or happy talk formats. Those few who actually tried to hang in there with hard-hitting political and religious talk formats would live in terror like members of Congress, facing reelection every even-numbered year, always looking over their shoulder, always trying to find a way to mollify another constituency.

None of this is our concern at the moment. This is not a book about how to stop the government from intimidating opposition voices; this is a book about how to survive and even prosper under the new rules.

I have a friend who owns several radio stations. We chat once or twice per year. He spends most of our time together griping about the regulatory environment. I try to change the subject to how his stations are doing. Since they're not doing very well, he changes the subject back to the adverse environment. Finally, I said to him, "Bob, it's time to get past all this. If you stay focused on the fairness of the rules, you'll stay obsessed with their unfairness. You'll have a stake in complaint about the problems rather than solving them. You have become emotionally dependent on the things that government tells you you're not allowed to do, as a distraction from the hard work of solving your business problems." Bob said that I was right and pledged to change his way of looking at the year. Our next semiannual conversation was, nevertheless, identical to all the others. I don't want you to be Bob.

Be like me. I got my start in media because of these regulations. The original radio and TV shows I hosted were designed to fulfill the public file requirements. I didn't shake anyone down or threaten to use the process against anyone. It's just that they had a requirement to provide community programming and I had the knowledge to do it. I was able to turn sewer bond issues and economic development issues into great issues of freedom or coercion. Scratch that; I didn't turn them into those bigger topics, I brought out the bigger topics that were in them all along but were buried under boring newsprint and municipal jargon.

The meager regulatory climate of the '80s and '90s created the opportunities for what became my career. The cornucopia of new rules out of D.C. will provide a new generation of media entrepreneurs with even more opportunities.


HERE ARE A few ideas:

Community Affairs Consulting: Talk radio is a giant industry. It will not go quietly into the dusk of broadcasting blandness. But it has many well-organized enemies. If talk radio opens the door to community input, the usual suspects will walk through it. But what if talk radio aggressively recruits and organizes its own natural constituencies? The Left has its race hustlers, class warriors, gender card players, and various special pleaders. But the right has its groups, too: megachurches, hunting clubs, gun owners, police associations, private schools, charter schools, antitax groups, and a myriad of business associations. We're the real grassroots deal; the Left is the Astroturf. They invent constituencies who exist only to the degree that they can come to the politicians and exchange endorsement for subsidy. The people who actually run real-life things from church boards to block watches are, as a rule, more conservative by far than the Astroturf identity politics imitations.

Talk radio speaks to the members of these groups, but ignores the groups themselves. Hosts speak not from ivory but from steel towers, out into the undifferentiated ether of "the audience." Perhaps it is time that promulgators of the philosophy that extols mediating institutions actually get to know some of them. Maybe it is time to ask for their help. How can we improve? If you like what we're doing, can you write letters of support? Can you circulate petitions on our behalf? Can you tell us the issues that are seeping up from the grassroots level, so that we can start working on them now? These are questions that people representing real community constituencies would like to hear.

Someone needs to help radio to do this. Maybe it's you. They will pay you for it; the stakes are too high not to.

And if they ignore the problem, maybe you might get a chance to try your hand at this yourself. Lots of stations are going to have to move away from political talk, even while the demand for it will be rising.

If you're not ready to run a station, how about running a show? As I said, that's how we got our start. You give the station a community-affairs-compliant show. Hit all the right themes; fill their public file with goodies. Sell your own ads and pocket the difference. It's a good small business model, and one that has worked for us.

Third, campaign finance reform will soon emerge as a tool

of regulating talk shows. In fact, it already has. As I write this book, I sit next to a pile of mail that includes a complaint filed with the Federal Election Commission. Our company produces radio and TV shows and one of our hosts interviewed a Republican candidate for Congress. It was a supportive interview. Shortly thereafter we and the host both received copies of a complaint filed with the federal government. The astonishing line of reasoning ran as follows: The host's positive comments constitute an endorsement; the endorsement is valuable to the candidate endorsed; therefore, the comments constitute an "in-kind contribution." Corporations are not allowed to make contributions; therefore, we have violated federal election law.

I called the Federal Election Commission to discuss the complaint. The lady at the complaint desk told me that she has been seeing a lot of this lately. This is political suppression (not so), pure and simple.

Will it work? A little. Like the fairness doctrine strategy outlined above, the use of campaign finance regulation as a tool of harassment will affect those most vulnerable to intimidation. Stations that have the heart for combat and the budget to get lawyered up will generally win. Stations that lack either one will react the way the meek always react to state bullying—they'll get out of the way.

Any form of communications is vulnerable to this form of control. The danger is not limited to spectrum broadcasters. A NASCAR driver was rebuked by the FEC for displaying "Bush/Cheney 2004" on his car. Even a sign on the side of a barn is considered fair game for regulation:

> . . . consider the case of Bill Liles, who faced an FEC inquiry when Smith was commissioner. In 2000, a businessman named Harvey Bass in the little Texas town of

Muleshoe painted "Save Our Nation: Vote Democrat Al Gore For President" on a beat-up box and plunked it on his furniture store's porch. Sick of looking at the sign, Liles and a friend pasted a "bigger and better" poster praising George W. Bush on a trailer and parked it right across from Bass's store. This was too much for another local, Don Dyer, who complained to the FEC that Liles's sign lacked the mandated disclosures about who paid for it and whether Bush has signed off on it.

—BRIAN ANDERSON AND ADAM THIERER,
*A Manifesto for Media Freedom*

Conventional talk shows will not be immune—indeed, are not immune:

> Consider what happened recently in Washington State as a warning. Early in 2005, the Democrat-controlled legislature passed, and Governor Christine Gregoire (also a Democrat) signed, a bill boosting the state's gasoline tax by a whopping 9.5 cents per gallon over the next four years, supposedly to fund transportation projects. Thinking that the taxes were already plenty high and that the state's corrupt Transportation Department would just squander the gas-tax revenues, some citizens organized an initiative campaign to junk the new levy, calling their effort No New Gas Tax.

—BRIAN ANDERSON AND ADAM THIERER,
*A Manifesto for Media Freedom*

The freedom of the press is supposed to be sacrosanct, as are other less celebrated liberties, such as the "right to petition the government for a redress of grievances." Media speaking out against an unpopular piece of legislation should be subject to multiple levels of constitutional protection.

Two popular conservative talk radio hosts, Kirby Wilbur and John Carlson, explained why the gas tax was bad news and urged listeners to supply the 225,000 petition signatures needed to get the rollback initiative on the November ballot, though they played no official role in the campaign and regularly featured defenders as well as opponents of the tax hike on their programs. With the hosts' help, the petition drive got almost twice the number of needed signatures; but the ballot initiative—strongly opposed by labor unions, the state's liberal media, environmental groups, and other powerful interests—narrowly lost.

Meantime, a group of pro-tax politicians sued No New Gas Tax, arguing that Wilbur's and Carlson's on-air commentaries were "in-kind contributions" and that the antitax campaign had failed to report them to the proper state authorities.

—BRIAN ANDERSON AND ADAM THIERER,
*A Manifesto for Media Freedom*

What does all of this mean to entrepreneurs and investors? It means a shift of value away from companies that evolved in an environment of full political freedom. It means serious costs imposed on conservative media outlets, such as syndicated talk radio and anything associated with Fox News. It means pressure on small AM radio stations. It means that you might have an opportunity to own one.

FM stations gravitate toward music. That's because FM is a much higher quality of sound. You don't need high fidelity to hear a human voice speaking, however, so talk radio has tended to be an AM radio phenomenon. This means that AM radio tends to offer a lot of religion and politics, and increasingly, alternate health content. The former two formats (and perhaps the latter) will come under increasing pressure to blunt their message. But the problem is that the audience doesn't want blunted messages. Many stations will be forced to shift formats, but to what? Music doesn't work on the AM band very well. Liberal opinion will already be offered in vast quantities by mainstream media. New formats will need to be created that cater to the audience's desire for strong content, but which can avoid the new media police.

I suggest two solutions:

Business news/talk is a newly emerging format that I have helped in some small ways to pioneer. A majority of Americans own investments. Market issues have moved to the very center of life on earth. In fact, I believe that what the state and its wars were to the twentieth century, the market and its disruptions are to the twenty-first. When the present turbulence passes, our interest in the market will not pass. The market is in the middle of things for the foreseeable future. Instead of Right versus Left, the balance in financial talk is bull versus bear. Instead of a focus on polemics, the format focuses on reporting the real-world consequences of good and bad policy. Though they will try, the Left will find it very difficult to regulate market commentators for describing shifts in currency and in-terest rates in reaction to anti-wealth policy proposals.

Documentaries are another end run around the media police. They don't require broadcast. You can view the free ones on YouTube, or buy inexpensive DVDs from Amazon. Soon you will be downloading them from iTunes. The state has no jurisdiction here. You can be as opinionated as you want to be and the FCC can't do a thing about it. You can sell your documentaries during an election season and, since people are purchasing them, it can't be designated an in-kind contribution. This latter threat is, unfortunately, not imaginary; it has already happened. The distributors of the anti-jihadist documentary *Obsession* mailed out millions of copies. A liberal group objected and the court sided with the liberal group, holding that since the documentary was not made by traditional documentarians it is not protected the same way that documentaries like those of Michael Moore are.

Documentary filmmaking is a bull market if ever I've seen one, but it is early in its development. This means the points of entry for wealth creation are not easy to find. I suggest two routes: production and financing.

The technology is available now to do professional-looking documentaries at relatively low cost. *Obsession* was made for roughly $400,000. Digital cameras and PC-based editing systems have pushed the cost of production to lower and lower levels. Production is still time-intensive, but not nearly as money-intensive as it used to be. This is the perfect environment for entrepreneurs. I especially like the idea of documentaries with regional appeal; the competition is not nearly as fierce as documentaries with national themes. Hometown pride tends to get regional productions a lot of earned media from local outlets and probably some free-play opportunities from local media. The failures of the Left at the local level, through giant social experiments, such as urban renewal, public housing, forced busing, educational fads, and so on, are just as heartbreaking as their national failure, and probably easier to document.

Regionally focused documentaries are a good place to learn the skills of documentary production. However, if you're looking for a baby step beforehand, try mini-documentaries, such as the ones you can find on YouTube. Numerous young conservatives have created and distributed ten- or fifteen-minute-long documentaries that have found a real following on the Internet. Much of the software is available in freeware versions at no cost, or at low cost. Start watching them and see what you can learn.

If you're a money person but not a creative one, try gathering some investors to put small amounts of money into a documentary production process. A limited partnership with, say, ten partners, putting in $50,000 apiece, could fund a very impressive documentary. Perhaps you can hold a contest with a $5,000 prize for a conservative short documentary, with the rights to develop the winner into a full-length project. That's where you get your talent pool. The contestant with the most promising work gets the money to expand it into something bigger. Get it listed on Amazon and other sites. Put teasers online with YouTube. Send review copies to local talk show hosts. Visit regional bookstores, video rental places, and grocery store chains, and ask them to put the documentary on the shelf. Send the producers out to speak at schools and civic groups. Sell them at a good markup and make a good profit. Learn what works and what doesn't, and do more of the former and less of the latter. Distribute the profits to your partners and move on to the next project.

DVD distribution is a high-margin business. By all means, save the world, but try to make at least 20 percent on the deal.

## The Political Bull Market

The world has slipped into a political bull market. Such a market is in some ways the opposite of a traditional bull market in which financial assets appreciate in value and government remains relatively stable. A political bull market is one in which politics itself grows, and the market suffers.

It's not just the election of Barack Obama as president of the United States that should concern you; the Congress had already moved to the left before the presidential election. And it's not just the Democrats. George Bush signed the Sarbanes-Oxley financial regulation bill and the McCain-Feingold campaign finance regulation bill. He promoted a Medicaid drug benefit, and acquiesced on alternative energy subsidies and auto fuel-efficiency mandates. He renewed the Community Reinvestment Act, and promoted a massive bailout to the banking industry, while neglecting any timely action to deal with the destructive effects of "fair value" accounting regulations. The shift to central planning began years before Obama, perhaps with the very birth of "compassionate conservatism."

This new politicization took much of the world, including yours truly, by surprise. We had gotten used to a post-Reagan world of the "American consensus," under which free-market capitalism was a settled conclusion. Even Democrats, such as Bill Clinton, seemed to have made their peace with the market. Like any triumphant kingdom, however, the capitalist system became complacent and left its gates unguarded.

This growth in the political sector is more than just a matter of increasing tax and regulatory costs: it is a matter largely of increased cost of calculation. Decisions become much more difficult any time you add a new dimension. The marketplace is complicated even in the simplest of times. But we are not in the simplest of times; we're in a time of rapidly expanding global trade. Challengers can come not just from any one of 300 million rival American entrepreneurs, but also from any of the 3 billion new capitalists who came online during the past decade.

Managing a business enterprise under globalist circumstances was already something like playing an incredibly intricate version of a 3-D Vulcan chess game. Add to that an outright assault from our own American political class and you've made business the most complicated career there is. Think 3-D chess but with rules that shift midgame whenever one of the players succeeds in lobbying the ref to change them. Oh, and if you inadvertently break one of the new rules or make a move that is not in the spirit of them, you don't just lose the game, you go to jail as well.

It doesn't help matters any that there is a talent shift from private to public careers that accompanies the shift in power to government. Government is now the hot career, and Washington, D.C., the hot boomtown. Washington is, after all, a company town. The company, in this case, is the federal government. Around that government cluster the vendors who live off of the crumbs that fall from the federal table—little golden crumbs. Manhattan lives off of finance; Dallas lives off of oil; Kansas City lives off of farming; Pittsburgh lived off of steel; San Diego lives off of technology; Hollywood lives off of pop culture; and Washington lives off of Manhattan, Dallas, Kansas City, Pittsburgh, San Diego, Hollywood, and every other city and town in the country. And when the federal government takes a larger share of wealth and control from the rest of us, all of D.C. grows.

THE POLITICAL BULL market is attracting a new generation of some of the best and brightest (well, the brightest, at least) to Washington, D.C. They felt guilty about the time they spent making money in finance or law because no one ever communicated to them the high nature of the entrepreneurial calling. They didn't think that wealth was moral, but they pursued it anyway.

> We don't know exactly what the Obama administration will look like, but we do know that it will be full of earnest workaholics. I think of it as the Organization Kids' coming of age. In the spring of 2001, before the national trauma of 9/11, David Brooks wrote an essay in the *Atlantic* vividly describing Princeton undergraduates as ambitious achievers who seemed strangely soulless. Far from the sloppy and slouchy undergrad rebels of his youth, these kids loved adults and authority, and their highest ambition was to climb the professional ladder.
>
> —REIHAN SALAM, "BULL MARKET IN POLITICS: THE 'ORGANIZATION KIDS' ARE FLOCKING TO D.C.," FORBES.COM

Salam correctly discerns the mood behind this new generation of activists. They have the convert's zeal for "change" driven by a need to atone for their time spent "like a spy behind enemy lines" in business. But they are unwilling to change classes, to downsize their wardrobe and dining habits, or to drive a used car or give up expensive health club memberships. They're still careerists, whose career is now based on ruining other people's careers, the kinds of people who they used to be. Their zeal is fueled, not diminished, by the time they spent in the private economy.

Government has always had the power, but they haven't always had the brains. For twenty years the government-versus-market war was always guys who wear $200 suits versus guys who wear $2,000 suits. The Men's Wearhouse guys could send you to jail, but your Armani guys could almost always outsmart them. But now, Obama has his own Armani army of change agents, activists, lobbyists, foundation execs, and trial lawyers. He even has tech guys. This fight is going to be a lot tougher than corporate America thinks it is.

You're probably wondering about now how you are going to make any money off of all of this. You are going to make money by helping the good guys. They are going to need quite a lot of help. They don't know it yet, but a couple of contributions to the Sierra Club always announced by a nice African-American man who works in their public affairs department is not going to do the trick anymore. Obama's army wants fundamental change. They didn't leave a fast track to partnership at Dewey, Cheatem, and Howe to nibble around the edges of our political system. They are utopians, and since "where your treasure is, there your heart will be also," they will get a lot more fanatical before they get less so.

Unfortunately for America, the next big business is going to be the lobbying business. Not just lobbying per se, but the entire persuasion-industrial complex: public relations, government relations, advocacy groups, and think tanks (increasingly difficult to distinguish), as well as the research and analysis that they all use, are the business side of the political bull market.

How do you cash in?

It's not really a stock story, but it is an entrepreneurial and perhaps a real estate one.

Many fortunes will be made over the next several years by people who influence the direction of public policy. The larger the role of government, the larger the money flows that depend on political decision makers. Politics itself has become a much larger business. Think about, for example, a $1 trillion stimulus package. Where will it go? Who will get the money? What will it be spent on? Who will decide what it will be spent on? Will it stay under federal control, or will governors and mayors make the final call?

A trillion dollars is a lot of money, but it is not an unrealistic estimate of the amount of new spending that we would see under an Obama New New Deal. Surely you can see that a lot of money has to be spent by people who hope to influence these decisions.

Let's start at the beginning: the election process. This past presidential election was far and away the largest, financially speaking, in American history. Forget all of that good-government goo about McCain-Feingold getting the money out of politics. That was pure political propaganda. We've had incomparably larger sums of money spent after campaign finance regulation than before. So who actually gets that money?

Consultants get the money. Media outlets get it. Pollsters get it. Political canvassers get it. Database managers get it. Direct mail firms get it. Local politicians get it. There is a vast network of migrant political workers who move from campaign to campaign. They come together, like movie people, to create a big production, and when it's done, they move on to the next one. Some of them decide to settle down for a while and take a staff job with their candidate, if he wins. After that, they can get a big job in corporate public relations or lobbying. So that's the career path: you volunteer for some campaigns, then work for some, then run some, then become a political appointee, then a lobbyist or a flack, or (if you're a top guy) a paid political pundit. If you really like the consulting thing, though, you can keep doing that for a long, long time.

Politics is a good career. Not just because Obama won. The general policy drift in the country is toward more politicization.

Even if Obama loses in 2012, the agents of "hope and change" are not going to pack up and go home. They're all in. In a ham and egg breakfast the chicken is involved, but the pig is committed. Well, Obama's army is committed.

This political industry is structurally decentralized. The typical political consulting firm is small; it has the guy's last name in the title. The proprietors of these firms are the typical blow-dried guy or power-suit-clad lady on TV repeating talking points. They're usually identified as "political consultants." They get paid by campaigns or parties to say the things they say.

This is not just a national thing; it's a local thing, as well, and the local part is going to get very important. In the end, infrastructure money comes to the state or municipality. Do you know your local political scene? Who is your governor? Good, I'm glad you know the answer. How about your congressman? Not so sure. County commissioner? Borough council? Water authority board member? The water guy oversees a rather large budget. Lawyers, engineers, bond underwriters, and others hang on his every word. Maybe you should learn a little about these people, too.

This is not an entrepreneurial opportunity into which you can leap with both feet. There is a steep learning curve. You have to actually know who these people are and what they do. They have to get to know you. You may actually have to volunteer for a campaign or two. Go where the lines are shortest; you'll get to the front faster. Start small and follow Elvis's advice—"stop, look and listen . . . it's called rubberneckin' baby, and it's alright with me." If you need money now, this is not for you. If you've already been involved, though, you might have a good head start.

Maybe you're not the entrepreneur; maybe you are the backer. Campaigns tend to be sprints; therefore, consulting tends to be a young man's game. Yes, I know you see gray-headed political consultants on TV, but that's the point, they're on TV. They're not running through the Allentown airport with two cell phones and a BlackBerry going at the same time while trying not to miss their connecting flight. The gray heads have earned the privilege of message crafting. New entrants have to do the sweaty work.

So, do you know any guys who are ready to start a political consultancy, fund-raising, direct mail, or get-out-the-vote-effort business? Are they good at it? Can they get clients? Are they honest? Do they need some start-up money? They'll need office space, not primo, but rehabbed industrial or loft space. Someone has to buy the computers, maybe a database, too, and staff. Capital is scarce right now, and the banks won't touch something as dicey as political consulting; it's too risky for them. Don't bet your retirement money on this one, but if you've got the right jockey, the business of politics is a pretty good horse. Don't do it alone; share the risk with a few other angel investors. Make the agreement ironclad—these guys can be slippery; even if they don't start that way, they'll learn it. Their earning power depends on personal access, so make sure you get a piece of everything they do, not just the direct campaign work.

The other opportunity is in media. Broadcast media is not an easy field to get into, but Internet media is quite easy. The only inevitable cost is the cost of learning. The world of political blogging is clogged at the top and anemic at the bottom. Everyone wants to tell you what they think about the auto bailout, but no one says a word about the sewer bonds.

But the sewer bonds are the hidden road to influence and wealth. Years ago, a friend of mine who ran a large FM talk radio station asked me to host his afternoon show. Okay, I said, but I want to talk about all sorts of different topics. This was an important point because the station was Christian format and they ran an all-religion-all-the-time lineup. He said I could talk about a wide range of topics, but "just don't talk about sewer bonds, okay?" He had listened to me hosting on other stations and, yes, along with Elian Gonzalez and Terri Schiavo and the Great Recount of AD 2000, I had discussed water and sewer finance.

One of my first guests was the very-well-known and influential new county executive. He came to the studio and the manager of the station was thrilled to meet him. The executive was an old friend of mine and was only too happy to drop by. "How did you get to know him, Jerry?" the station manager asked. "Sewer bonds," I said. I had written a hard-hitting article about corruption surrounding the issuance of sewer bonds, which came to the country executive's attention and we became friends over it.

My article had not been published in the newspaper, or even printed by me. I distributed my analysis pieces by fax (later by e-mail). The only cost was the time spent learning the issues. It's easier now with the Internet than it was when I did it.

So what can you do to get started? You can read the municipal section of the newspaper. You can write a blog. You can send out position papers to influential people. You can send letters to the editor. You can submit op-eds to local newspapers. You can volunteer to discuss these issues on local radio. You can build a local mailing list. Get involved with the League of Women Voters or other civic forums. Attend open government meetings. Be helpful, not nutty. Before you open your mouth, make sure you know what you are talking about. Before long, you'll begin to see opportunities to make yourself useful. You will notice services that need to be performed for which people will pay. Campaign work, such as get-out-the-vote efforts, is valuable to politicians, as is managing databases of voters. Political fund-raising is a growing field. If you can gather people who are willing to help fund a politician, you are a valuable commodity.

If your blog or newsletter or, eventually, radio or TV program develops a politically influential following, advertisers will come. Not just campaigns, though during the political season they spend a lot of money. Go for advocacy groups, too, especially in the off-season. Don't forget the business community, which is so vulnerable to changes in government policy.

Let's talk more about this last category. The Left is in charge and they're going to assault businesses. Businesses need help. They'll need people who can deliver their message to the general public, to the state capital, and to Washington. They'll need a lot of public relations work done. PR is sometimes done by giant firms, but a lot of PR is done by little guys. I hear from PR firms every day. They pitch guest ideas to us because we produce some radio and TV shows. Most of them are small, a lady (usually) and a couple of low-paid people who basically work the phone banks. They send e-mails to us and follow up by phone. Most of them get paid by the number of bookings they generate for their clients.

An age of gotcha politics and gotcha journalism is an age in which the need for corporate communications will grow rapidly. Perhaps you have the skill set to start a business along those lines.

The real estate side of the political bull market is a good deal more complicated, and needs more specialized attention than I can give here. Real estate is an illiquid and highly regionalized industry. Generally you don't have a good or a bad national real estate market, but a patchwork of markets rising and falling relative to one another. A big part of the trick is to spot the ones that will rise before other people do. That's not the whole trick. You don't buy shares in a regional market, you buy a specific piece of property with specific terms. I can't help you choose the parcel or negotiate the price, but I can suggest the promising markets. Take a close look at political centers. I'm not just talking about the D.C. metro area but about Harrisburg, Albany, and Sacramento, as well. In an age of ascendant liberalism, these capital cities tend to rise in wealth relative to other cities. The money flows through their budgets rather than through private markets. This new money means new staff, and new influencers trying to wine and dine that staff. When the market has the upper hand, market towns like Manhattan, Chicago, or Silicon Valley thrive. When government has the upper hand, political cities thrive. This is not good for the country. Centers of government tend to become parasitical cities, recession-proof, in fact booming when the rest of us are scraping bottom. But there it is and you can take advantage of it if you are smart.

It's tough to build in places like that; influence is needed. You can buy things already built, or go lower risk and look at parking space, a small lot near the capitol, for instance. Maybe a cab service would make sense, although those are notoriously political in most cities. Restaurants are a high-risk bet, more like base jumping than like business, but catering is less chancy. Media, too. Typically, there are a few small AM radio stations in any capital city. Are they for sale? Is their all-religion or all-Afrocentric programming working for them during an economic downturn? If buying a radio station is biting off more than you can chew, perhaps buying a few hours of airtime per week is something you can swallow. Focus on budget and regulatory issues, get political advertisers. Cross-promote with blast e-mails and newspaper op-eds.

Again, let me reiterate something important: This kind of investing takes a lot of due diligence. But remember to look for the big waves—capital cities look like promising places to surf the socialism.

## Planes, Trains, Automobiles, and Other Suckers' Bets

In an era when the central political authority makes most of the decisions about where to steer capital, it is tempting to try to find the next gravy train and hop on. Resist that temptation. It's a suckers' bet.

The current mood of the political class is very much in favor of bailouts: Republicans do it for banks; Democrats do it for unionized heavy industry. The people hate it, but the people aren't really in charge for the moment; interest groups are. So why not buy into an AIG or a GM in anticipation of the government checks? Because the bailout isn't for your benefit; it's for the interest groups. Government doesn't bail out a GM to protect the shareholders. It bails out a GM to give aid and comfort to the United Auto Workers. The shareholders, despite being victimized by big-taxing governments, pro-union arbitrators, and environmental fanatics, will play the role of the villain. The angrier the populists are about the bailouts, the more the villains are needed. Villain number one: the shareholder class. The shareholders are the virgins that get thrown into the volcano. Maybe the plague will pass, but don't count on it. You don't want to be the politically unprotected class during a bailout. The unions elect Democrats. The managers donate to Republicans. Small shareholders haven't paid their protection money; therefore, they are unprotected.

Expect to see a lot of smart-bomb subsidies in the near future. Money to banks—but they must lend it out to troubled borrowers, not give it to management or to the owners. We'll be told over and over again that we should not "reward the guilty," as though lending money to someone who refuses to pay it back is the morally suspect side of the transaction. Give money to automakers, but it has to go to the "workin'" man, even though giving too much money to labor is what got the Big Three into trouble in the first place. Money will be given to insurers, but the shareholders who actually took the risk will be wiped out.

It won't just be bailouts; it will be massive subsidies to favored industrial groups. Public transit will get massive infusions of taxpayer money. Troubled airlines will get help, as well. Avoid these investments. The deck is stacked against you and toward the political constituencies that are important to the left coalition: civil service bureaucracies; public and private sector unions; politically connected financial players, and so on. Private investors are there to give the illusion of market legitimacy to subsidy/bailout/mandate. Once they are no longer needed, they will be sheared and dismissed. There is a highly complex system of political information gathering, and unless you are right in the middle of it, you are wise to stay out of the world of public-private partnerships, which are tilted toward the former and against the latter.

There is an exception to the rule about avoiding investments in bailed-out industries: bonds. To understand why, you must first understand more about how the bailout economy works.

In the normal course of business affairs, when a company finds that it can no longer keep the promises it has made to its lenders and its employees, it files for bankruptcy. That's what bankruptcy is for. It is an exception to the general principle of the sanctity of contracts. It is intended to be invoked only when it is simply impossible for a company to pay its debts. This may not seem fair to most Americans, and certainly doesn't seem fair to the lenders, but there is simply no alternative. If a company doesn't have the money, then it doesn't have the money. Bankruptcy is the legal and financial recognition that life is not fair.

But even in bankruptcy, there is some justice. Lenders are given something, when it's possible to do so. Secured creditors, who were more provident in their investment decisions, get assets. If the company has reasonable prospects, it is allowed to restructure and continue operating and perhaps pay back most of its obligations after a period of relief.

Last in line is the shareholder, as he should be. He's the owner; he ultimately was in charge; he had the most to gain, and therefore he should have the most to lose. That's why I told you in the section above not to be the shareholder in a failing business.

If bankruptcy holds all these wonderful tools, why does government do bailouts at all? All too often, our leaders refuse to let companies enter into bankruptcy because they show political favoritism to one of the groups from which the company seeks relief. More often than not, that group is a collective bargaining unit of a labor union.

Congress and the administration won't let a big auto company go to bankruptcy if they can help it because in bankruptcy everyone is forced to face the reality that they made a poor decision and they are not going to be able to get everything they want. Congress is perfectly happy to let vendors and shareholders and consultants and any other group take their chances before a bankruptcy trustee, but not the UAW. Their contracts, and their contracts alone, are sacrosanct.

We saw this in the recent episode regarding the Chrysler Corporation. The administration went to extraordinary, historically unprecedented measures in an extended game of chicken with the bondholders. Were it not for the fact that a large proportion of those bondholders also happened to be, at the same time, large TARP (Troubled Asset Relief Program) recipients under implied threat of nationalization, the bondholders would have remained in control of the situation. Still, even with the amazing level of political threats, it is likely as of this writing that the investors who bought those bonds at the height of the crisis will get a reasonable return.

There are lessons to be learned from the Chrysler situation. First, don't underestimate the lengths to which the Left is willing to go in order to reward their friends and hurt their enemies. Traditional constitutional restraints are cut through like tissue paper when a union is in trouble and a bank is holding out. If you are depending on the rule of law, make sure you are counting on some branch of government over which President Obama has little power. Bankruptcy courts are generally not as politicized as other segments of the judiciary. They have a long history of dealing with contract law. The other lesson is to be careful about whom you choose to have in the foxhole next to you. Make sure that the other distressed bondholders are not in the government-punishment seat. If they are, for instance, TARP recipients, they'll fold. There will be no traditional bankruptcy. The shareholders will be wiped out. The bondholders will be partially wiped out; and you won't have the redress of a bankruptcy court, because you will have less than the customary 5 percent stake that gets you a seat at the table. Make sure you've got strong allies, who add up to far more than the 5 percent stake and who can't be waterboarded into giving up their money. It should help quite a lot if the decision makers are also the owners. In other words, if the people at the table are hirelings, gambling with someone else's money, they'll scatter when the wolf comes. Mixed metaphors aside, you want to be in the foxhole with other owners, ornery, honorable other owners. Get this mix and you might find some opportunities for enormous upside. This is high-risk trading; do a lot more due diligence over it than just reading this chapter before you enter into something like this.

So where does all of this leave bondholders? In the cat-bird seat, that's where. Since bonds are a debt instrument, and not an ownership instrument like stocks, the bondholders are creditors. They therefore have the power to force a company into bankruptcy. If a certain critical mass of debt holders calls for bankruptcy, then it must happen. In the case of autos, airlines, utilities, and any of the other large, old-line, industrial clients who are likely to appear in line at the Treasury soup kitchen, the creditors will tend to be bondholders. They hold the bankruptcy detonator. If they push it, the whole bailout blows up and the politically connected unions find themselves in line with everybody else. Congress won't let that happen, so they will bail out the industry and make sure the bondholders are paid and happy.

## Get Real (Estate)

It probably sounds like I'm nuts, but I think you should begin to look at real estate as an investment again. That wave of anxiety you just felt, that's your lizard brain that makes you feel that way. Human beings are wired so that when they go through a traumatic experience, they continue to feel a stab of emotional pain every time they encounter anything that reminds them of the original trauma. If you have the flu, and don't know it, and grab a sausage sandwich on your way home from work, and then get sick later that evening, you'll hate sausages for a while.

You'll hate the way they smell; you'll hate the word "sausage"; you'll wince when you see a sausage vendor on the street.

So America, not knowing that it was already ill, grabbed a giant steaming piece of real estate, slapped it on a bun, swallowed it whole, and then got sick. It hates residential real estate; it hates commercial real estate; it hates Real Estate Investment Trusts (REITs). It hates mortgage banks, companies that insure mortgages, and companies that insure the companies that insure mortgage banks. This is the damage that comes from unanalyzed pain.

Scientists call the part of your cerebellum that registers that negative stimulus and response bond your "lizard brain." I don't like the expression much; I prefer the classical view of man's mind as divided between parts that correspond to head, heart, and stomach, the tripartite or "triptych" view of the human soul.

To borrow from Plato, the soul is divided into three parts: reason, conscience, and appetite, corresponding to head, heart, and belly, respectively. A man controlled by appetites avoids pain at all costs, and seeks pleasure above all. He avoids work because it makes him sweat. He eats and drinks whatever he wants because it feels good. In the long run, sloth and gluttony lead to poverty and illness, but Appetite Man doesn't live in the long run.

Reason Man, however, does live in the long run. He analyzes his pain, studies the cause-and-effect patterns that led him to his trauma. He adjusts his passions to his rational faculties and adjusts his rational faculties to objective reality. Over time he becomes habituated to what is true and good and beautiful; this becomes the basis of his character. These fundamental truths are the foundation of all human endeavors, including investment. Those who ignore the basics of human nature, especially the basic flaws of their own nature, will wait too long to invest in out-of-favor sectors, and they will stay too long in irrationally favored sectors. I would say that this problem is probably the basis of more investment mistakes than any other. In that sense, you should take it into account as you read every part of this book. But the phenomenon is likely to be most damaging, at the moment, in real estate investment.

A strong real estate investment environment needs three things: good fundamental demographics, widely available credit, and people whose income is adequate to qualify for credit. The current crisis lacked, more than anything else, the second condition. Our recent housing bust was not caused by a famine, plague, or war. We did not see mass movements of refugees who left behind millions of empty houses. Fertility and life expectancy rates are stable and improving, respectively. The main problem is that the credit market froze. The first sector to be affected was the sector most directly dependent on credit—housing. The second sector to be affected was the one that was almost as dependent on credit—autos. Then durable goods, maybe school loans, and so on. This was not a real estate crisis causing a banking crisis. It was a banking crisis causing a real estate crisis. Can any serious person still believe that all of this—the global meltdowns, the wild currency swings, the failed and nationalized banks, the global panic, and all the rest—was caused by default on a small fraction of smaller-than-average homes in a few lower-middle-class neighborhoods in America? It started with subprime adjustable rate mortgages, because they were the most vulnerable to tight credit. Subprime mortgages were the canary in the coal mine. The gas kills them first because they are the weakest ones. Then it kills the miners. Or perhaps you would prefer to believe the alternate theory—that dead canaries emit a virus that is fatal for coal miners. This theory of real estate and credit markets has dominated the financial coverage of our current crisis from the beginning. Commentators tell us that there is a financial "contagion" that spread from subprime mortgages to prime mortgages and then to the whole credit market. But what exactly is a financial contagion? How does it spread? Did the adjustable rate mortgage market engage in openmouthed kissing with the fixed-rate market? What precisely is the vector of the contagion? What is the agent?

Some of us argued from the beginning that the subprime mortgage market was simply not large enough to cause much damage. That may have been misinterpreted as a belief that there really was no problem at all. But there was a problem and we knew it. By analogy, the problem was not the little canary. He didn't kill all those miners, he just felt it first. The problem was a set of misguided regulations that severely disrupted credit markets, killing off credit-sensitive sectors of the economy in order from most vulnerable to least.

But this will not last.

First, the Federal Reserve has created completely unprecedented quantities of new money and pumped that new money through a wide variety of old and newly created channels. The Fed has never been this aggressive in its history. It has roughly doubled the money supply in approximately one year. It has pumped so much money into the system that the Fed funds rate (the rate at which banks lend to one another for short periods) has plunged to approximately zero. It has opened the discount window, which is the part of the bank that lends directly to troubled banks, to nearly every variety of lending institution and has pressured even the healthy ones to borrow there so as to remove the stigma associated with using that facility. It has lent money based on a wide variety of securities that it has never before in its history accepted for such purposes. It has pledged to do more, as much as is needed, whatever is needed from its literally infinitely expandable balance sheet.

The money flood must be felt; it's only a question of when.

I think it will be felt soon. As of this writing, the deflationary signs have all reversed themselves. Raw materials, import prices, export prices have all ceased their plunges, as has the dollar. Some people have mistakenly concluded that for some reason the historically universal link between central bank money creation and available liquidity has been mysteriously broken. These people are confused because they have failed to see the distinction between money in existence and money in circulation. The Fed decides how much money exists. The banks decide how much money is to be circulated. If the Fed creates money and pumps it into the banks, the banks can either leave it there in idle pools of noncirculating liquidity or they can lend it out, and as the velocity returns to normal the supply of money in circulation begins to catch up on the supply of money in existence. Deflation ends.

Second, even under normal circumstances banks have an incentive to lend. They don't make money unless they turn around and lend it at interest. That is their function. But these are not normal circumstances; the large money-center banks have accepted large sums of taxpayer dollars, which have been appropriated to them by the United States Congress precisely in order to get the banks lending again. So, on top of the normal *market* pressure to lend, and grow market share and make a profit on their lending, the banks are under enormous *political* pressure to begin lending again, too.

They will lend, or else. Yes, there are a few old stick-in-the-mud regulators who want the banks to hold on to the cash as a capital cushion, but the overwhelming drift of political opinion is toward one direction: let's get the party started again—no more hoarding—let's stimulate spending and let's get it done yesterday.

This is bad news for taxpayers, but it is great news for real estate investors. Remember, our objective here is to surf the socialism. This hysterical level of money creation will almost certainly lead to a disruptive wave of inflation. The taxpayer bailouts of the banks have already led to their de facto nationalization. Credit will flow to the most politically potent borrowers, not the most economically potent ones. The stimulus plan will severely strain U.S. fiscal health. None of these things are good. And I don't want any of them to happen, and neither do you. But it would be foolish to pretend that we don't know what will happen and it would be equally foolish to ignore these plain political realities in our investment decisions.

Somewhere between 60 percent and 70 percent of U.S. households are home owners. There is no way that in the new environment of hyperpoliticized credit markets those voting citizens can be left off the gravy train. The government will do what it takes to keep their home prices from falling further, and will keep the credit flowing for them to sell their current house and to buy their next one, even if that means turning the banks into wards of the state.

So, HOW DO you make money?

There are varying levels of risk and commitment, ranging from instruments in which you can invest with the click of a mouse to direct involvement in commercial real estate development (or more likely, redevelopment).

Let's start with the easiest moves.

Firms that specialize in goods pertaining to home purchasing and improvement are well known. Lowe's and Home Depot are both well-established companies, with good consumer brands, and are easily accessible to investors as publicly traded companies.

Home builders, such at Toll Brothers, are market leaders in this area. Of course, whenever you engage in individual stock picking you need to investigate the company carefully on your own, and you should seek the counsel of your financial advisor. One way to mitigate the company-specific risks of buying shares of stock directly is to purchase a mutual fund that focuses in on a specific industry, like home building. In this way, you are placing a bet on the entire home-building and related industry, but not on a specific company and its management, regional focus, balance sheet, legal and regulatory vulnerabilities, and brand strength.

REITs are investments that apply the mutual fund to real estate. A traditional mutual fund is a company that owns the stock of other companies. So, when you buy a share of a Dow Jones Industrial Average (DJIA) mutual fund, you are buying a share in a company that owns shares in the companies that make up the Dow Jones in the proportions that they appear in that average. It's a nice, convenient prepackaged way to get what you want in one transaction rather than tracking down all thirty members of the DJIA and calculating how much of them to buy in which proportions to mimic the investment returns of the index itself. Mutual funds also do this with bonds and commodities and a dizzying myriad of sliced and diced and packaged combinations of stocks and bonds according to size and sector.

Real Estate Investment Trusts are investments that have harnessed one particular form of mutual fund, the "trust" structure, in order to make real estate investments as easy to purchase as stock investments. The tax treatments are essentially the same, in that the income "flows through" the trust to the individual investor, and has the same characteristics when it does. In other words, the money that the REIT makes in the form of capital gains is treated as a capital gain to the REIT share owner. Ditto for interest and ordinary income.

REITs are the broadest way for you to grab a piece of the general real estate pie. If you want to purchase real estate in a specific location, then you purchase it directly. If you want to buy into a growing mortgage market, then you can buy into the companies that are in that line of business. If you want to buy into the housing construction business, then you can buy mutual funds dedicated to home builders. But if you want to purchase real estate in a diversified form without spending large sums of money for a wide array of parcels around the country, then REITs are the right answer. The risks are lower, by and large, than direct real estate purchases, and consequently the rewards are lower.

The main limitation with REITs is that they are overwhelmingly focused on commercial property. That makes sense: Commercial property is often owned by large real estate development companies, which then lease space to various commercial tenants. Residential real estate is not quite as conducive to the REIT structure. As I write this, I believe that residential housing has bottomed and has begun its reascent, but that commercial property has more trouble ahead.

Here is what I recommend as of the time of this writing: REITs focused on residential real estate for middle-class owners broadly distributed nationally with, if available, a focus on metropolitan regional areas. Residential REITs, as I said above, are hard to find, but worth looking for. The current residential options tend to be assisted-living facilities and apartment complexes. These are promising, but not optimal. What you really want is something that focuses on single-family dwellings, which, unfortunately, are not available at the moment. Why do I recommend an investment that does not exist? Because new investment products are released all the time. New mutual funds, REITs, and exchange-traded funds (ETFs) appear every week. By the time you read this, there is a reasonable chance that there will be better REITs available.

My real estate recommendation is the result of a political, not an economic, choice. By this I mean that residential real estate investment would not be nearly as good a bet if not for the political environment. The desirability of subsidies to home ownership is pretty much as close to a bipartisan consensus as any bad idea can be. Democrats want houses for single moms and minorities and small tofu manufacturers. Republicans want them for everyone else. In this kind of environment, subsidies breed subsidies. That is, when subsidized markets falter, the state doubles down on the subsidy. What it learns from its mistakes is that the mistakes weren't big enough.

When the credit markets unfreeze, and when home buyers and investors conclude that they have waited long enough for prices to fall to absolute rock bottom, then the housing market will explode upward. The recent housing crisis represents a deferral of demand, not a destruction of it. People didn't stop reproducing, and they didn't stop earning (for the most part), and they didn't stop dreaming of a two-car garage. They just stopped buying houses. If you think of the housing sector as a movie, then think of America as having pushed the "pause" button on the story of American home purchasing; it did not push the "eject" button.

For people who have the requisite special skills to direct real estate investing, things could be very promising right now.

Those people know better than anyone else precisely which neighborhoods have been the most artificially depressed by a temporary mortgage market distortion. In other words, those markets that have the greatest pent-up demand based on solid demographic and economic fundamentals are the ones that have the most catching up to do when the mortgage market becomes functional again. Those markets are the most irrationally undervalued. Geography is critical in this calculation. Booming areas tend to be located near booming industries, or at least those saved from destruction. Depressed neighborhoods near politically favored industries are high-reward (though high-risk) bets. Upper-middle-class autoworker neighborhoods are a target-rich environment. So are university towns. Financial worker upscale neighborhoods will not be. In that case, those employees are the wrong party registration and therefore expendable, and are left politically unprotected from layoffs. Farmworker neighborhoods are a mixed bag. Traditional farm subsidies will probably be cut in order to free up tax money for more green energy. So don't look for real estate opportunities there.

The green agenda means there must be increasingly high energy prices, and inflation will accelerate that trend. This means that the "carbon Americans"—those people who work with oil, coal, and natural gas—will be increasingly in demand. However, coastal drilling is an exception to the general bull market in energy. I recommend that you don't look for boomtowns in disputed continental shelf areas. Though offshore drilling is technically legal, the Obama administration will block new offshore drilling through endless permitting hurdles.

It should go without saying that real estate is scarcer in towns in which government is the big industry. The D.C. metro area will boom as government booms. New lobbyists, new staffers, new and bigger houses for better-paid federal bureaucrats are the order of the day. Ditto for state capitals, especially in swing states.

This isn't just a residential play; it is a commercial one, as well. Towns populated by people who work for government or by people who influence the people who work for government will do well under Obama. The federal workforce is recession-proof; in fact, it is counter-recessionary. And federal employees are insulated from inflation with cost-of-living adjustments that are larger than inflation itself. As tragic as it may be for me to say this, the great race for the next several years will not be the race to design the fastest microchip, or the most lifesaving drug, or the next great deposit of oil. For the time being, the great race is the race to divvy up several trillion dollars in stimulus and bailout money. Large quantities of that wealth are being captured in new real estate development in edge cities near political power centers, in homes in industrial parks filled with the doctors, dentists, and accountants who serve the residents of those homes, and in trendy retail centers where they all shop.

At the moment retail real estate is still headed toward a crash. Circuit City is gone, the first victim of the tech chain store massacre, in which a rampaging deflation has crushed the profit margins of much of the electronics business. Others will follow. As deflation continues, more and more retailers have been pushed to the edge, will destroy their balance sheets trying to avoid going over it, and eventually be swept across it and down into bankruptcy. Bad news for them; good news for retail space purchasers. Buyers who have kept their powder dry, their credit good, and their eyes open are able to purchase the big boxes in which big box retailers formerly operated, just in time for an inflation-fueled retail recovery. You don't have to be the next great idea in retailing; you don't even have to know what the next great idea in retailing is. You just have to buy near the bottom and sell (or lease) to the business that has the next great idea. Retail spending will return, because inflation will return, and when inflation appears people stop deferring their purchase decisions. They say to themselves, "Buy now before it goes up in price."

How do you invest in retail real estate? If you're a big guy, you just buy the building. If you are a medium-sized guy, you do it through a real estate partnership. It's a deal-specific thing, not something you can do in an open market, like buying General Motors stock. You talk to your accountant or your attorney if his firm is big enough to have a commercial real estate specialist. This is an area in which you should really kick the tires. I'm giving you the concept. Each deal is different.

# CHAPTER EIGHT

# The Bush Boom, Bust, and a New Birth of Freedom

Sometime around the year 1999 my son, Jeremy, asked me to teach him about economics. Since he was in his early teens at the time, I started him with the basics. I assigned Henry Hazlitt's classic *Economics in One Lesson*, which is a collection of popular essays written by the former economic columnist for *Newsweek*. Next, I gave Jeremy Thomas Sowell's future classic, *Basic Economics*, and then Frederick Bastiat's *The Law*. Being a bright lad, Jeremy quickly learned the principles and as quickly learned to articulate them. When the time came to take this basic education, expressed in English prose, and transform it into a deeper understanding expressed in mathematics, we turned to current data releases. I told Jeremy that every day one or more pieces of important data are released from some public or private agency. Durable goods orders, monthly deficit estimates, unemployment rates, inflation, gross domestic product, and so on are quantified, compiled, graphed, and sent out into the world every morning. I told Jeremy that we don't have to wait until the next morning to see this information dumbed down for us in print, that ordinary citizens can now get the full data releases via e-mail at exactly the same time as the press. Constrained by the cost of printing, newspapers report these numbers, but generally only in the most superficial ways. Often the most important numbers remain unreported, and the least important numbers appear in the headline of the story. Just as often, the articles contain "commonplaces"—that is, assertions that are false but widely believed because they are widely repeated. I told Jeremy that we can skip the filtering process altogether and go *ad fontes*, to the sources, and get the data unspun by the media. Jeremy and I began to test the commonplaces against the data. For example, it is hard to find an article about trade deficits (the amount by which imports of goods and services exceed exports of goods and services) that does not contain the commonplace that trade deficits cause the dollar to weaken against other currencies. I had already explained to Jeremy the theoretical problems with the trade deficit–weak dollar link, which appear with even minimal applications of reason. But what happens in the real world, we asked, when trade deficits rise and fall? The only way to see is to run the numbers. So on the day the quarterly trade deficit numbers appeared, we downloaded them to a spreadsheet and plotted them against a set of numbers showing how the dollar rose and fell in value in comparison with other currencies. We tested the commonplace. Like the emperor Balthazar in the imperial palace on the eve of the fall of Babylon, the commonplaces of economic reporting were weighed in the balance and found wanting. Budget deficits cause high interest rates, tax cuts cause deficits, growth causes inflation, recessions cause deflation, consumer sentiment drives the economy, and the rest were found again and again to be blatantly implausible when tested against the numbers.

I told Jeremy that the word "data" is Latin for the word "givens" or, as I prefer, "gifts." Data is the gift of insight; it is the gift of being able to test our presuppositions and to reject the ones that are disproved.

Jeremy ran the graphs, under my supervision, and I wrote up the two-paragraph commentaries. I was enjoying teaching my son economics and he was enjoying a rather extensive education for a fifteen-year-old. One day I sent a copy of one of these graph-commentary combos to Chris McEvoy at National Review Online. Chris told me that Larry Kudlow was going to be discontinuing his popular "BuzzCharts" column to focus more on his television career. He said that Larry would become editor of the financial section of the publication, and that Chris would show Larry my stuff and see if he would approve me as his successor. After a look at my material and a fascinating (for me) phone conversation, Larry gave me the thumbs-up. This would be the first of many acts of risky kindness from Mr. Kudlow to me and mine. I had been a huge fan of Kudlow already and was thrilled at the prospect.

Jeremy and I churned out dozens, even scores of BuzzCharts and, over time, a pattern emerged: With the election of George Bush, the coverage of the economy took a negative slant that did not accord with the actual data. The headlines were more bleak than the articles and the articles were more bleak than the actual data.

Furthermore, the policy mix had begun to shift by 2003 in a far more positive direction. Bush's 2001 tax cuts had been anemic at best. Lacking a core understanding of and commitment to free market economics, President Bush had negotiated away all of the elements of his campaign's tax-cut pledges to which the Left had objected. Bush had run on a promise to cut tax rates for every bracket of taxpayers, including a reduction of the top rate from 39.6 percent down to 35 percent. Democrats predictably complained about "tax cuts for the rich" and President Bush compliantly threw the rich under the bus, agreeing to defer the tax cuts for that bracket several years into the future. In essence, Bush caved to populism by giving tax cuts to the poor and middle class only. Adding insult to injury, the anemic results and "jobless recovery" were blamed on the very supply-side economics that Bush rejected. At the time, I wrote an article for the *New York Sun*, the title of which speaks for itself: "Partial Supply Side Policy Results in Partial Recovery," published on August 2, 2002.

By the spring of 2003, the weak economy had become such a political albatross that the White House was ready to take action. According to my sources, the impetus for genuine supply-side tax cuts came from the vice president's office. The plan that emerged called for immediate implementation of the cuts in the tax rates that had hitherto been deferred into the distant future. The plan also called for a cut in capital gains taxes, which ultimately was modified to include a cut for dividend taxes as well.

It became clear to us that the economy, which had been hobbling along with a relatively unexciting recovery, was going to kick into high gear. I decided in the midst of a press climate that kept referring to "the worst economy since Herbert Hoover" to publish a book that pointed to the clear evidence in the data that the new pro-growth policies were already leading to a boom. Since I didn't have time to write a book from scratch, I used columns to build one, cutting and pasting, modifying and augmenting them into a short book titled *The Bush Boom*. I began to call friends who were involved to one degree or another in the publishing industry to gauge their level of interest in publishing it. The first one I talked to said that it was a great idea; that the market would welcome a satirical book about how badly Bush had handled the economy. When I told him that the book was, in fact, not satire, I was greeted with a prolonged and awkward silence at the other end of the line. I became convinced that although we were on the verge of an exploding stock market, home prices, small business start-ups, and job creation, the world was stuck on "worst since Hoover" and that I would have to publish this book myself. My wife and I discussed it with each other, and with our children, and then we bowed our heads and discussed it with our Maker. In the end, we took out a second mortgage on our house and used it to publish *The Bush Boom: How a Misunderestimated President Fixed Our Broken Economy*.

You can imagine the reaction from traditional media and from the blogosphere. But there was another reaction from investors and small business owners around the country who had themselves seen in their daily lives the signs of turnaround. Despite the Left-baiting title, I was aware of and wrote about the areas of vulnerability in the economy. I suggested that the administration's decision to cave in on Sarbanes-Oxley, ramping up financial regulation, adding thousands of pages to the *Federal Register*, would in the end prove to be a mistake. I mentioned, also, the administration's tendency to manipulate currency markets in a mistaken attempt to lessen trade deficits as a serious threat to the boom in an article titled "Lowering the Boom," published on December 2, 2003, in the *New York Sun*.

In 2004, when it was clear that the Fed was going to stand by its loose money policy, I published an article titled "Stop the Presses" (November 26, 2004) in the *New York Sun*, in which I argued that a far too easy money creation policy from the Fed would lead to bubbles and inflation.

At the time, Paul Krugman and many of the editorial pages of liberal newspapers were still in high panic mode, arguing that tax cuts would not lead to growth and that the Fed needed to print more money. To my knowledge none of those people has publicly acknowledged the connection between the loose monetary policy they recommended and the severe credit cycle that resulted. Instead, most of them have posited some nonspecified causal link between a subprime housing market bubble and a tax cut that did not even include houses or the home-building industry.

The very week the book came off the presses, a shocking piece of data was released: the economy had grown by an astonishing 7 percent in the summer of 2003 (later revised up to over 8 percent)—the boom had begun.

You'll be glad to know that we did not lose our house, that we paid off the second mortgage, then paid off the first mortgage, and then sold the house and used the proceeds to make a large down payment on our "dream house." The book led to many good things for us, and the economy and investment markets showed extremely good results for the four years following its publication.

For the Bowyers the book led to a rather close relationship with the administration. Over the years I had on- and off-air conversations with Vice President Dick Cheney and his wife, Lynne, Secretary of State Condoleezza Rice, Secretary of Defense Donald Rumsfeld, Secretary of the Treasury John Snow, Secretary of Labor Elaine Chow, Secretary of Housing Alphonso Jackson, Secretary of Energy Sam Bodman, Secretary of Transportation Norm Mineta, Secretaries of the Navy John Lehman and Gordon England, Chief of Staff Josh Bolton, presidential advisors Karl Rove and Karl Zinsmeister, and chairman of the president's Council of Economic Advisors Ed Lazear. I was permitted to do two radio broadcasts live from the White House and one live from the Treasury Department. I informally advised the White House on many matters pertaining to economic policy, participated in dozens of conference calls with senior White House and Treasury officials, and had a number of memos around the White House.

Investors who bought in on the eve of the tax cuts, or even at the time when the book was published, would have seen their Dow Jones holdings skyrocket from the high 7,000s to the low 14,000s. Those who bought real estate at the time of the tax cuts would have seen similar growth rates. All told, the period ranging from 2003 to 2007 saw literally tens of trillions of dollars of new wealth added to the national balance sheet.

But all good booms must come to an end, not because markets fail to sustain them but because Washington kills them.

In this particular case, I've found three bullets at the scene of the crime. They are (in ascending order or caliber):

First, the expiration of the first of the Bush tax cuts, not in 2011, but at the end of 2007. In addition to the big tax cuts for income-tax payers and the cuts in the capital gains and dividend tax rates, the package passed in 2003 included powerful tax breaks for small business owners. These small business tax benefits got almost no attention from the press, but hundreds of thousands of CPAs sat down with millions of small business owners and told them that if they were going to purchase durable goods, such as cars, trucks, and high-end information equipment, they had better do it before December 2007, when those particular tax breaks would expire. Our CPA certainly did.

While the political class and their press penumbra were blathering on about the Bush tax cuts being safe until they expire at the end of 2011, the people who actually sat down and ran businesses every day knew that the first of the expirations occurred at the end of 2007. Not surprisingly, there was a spike of last-minute durable goods purchasing just before the expiration, and a plunge immediately following the expiration. If I told you that you could deduct all of the cost of a company car if you did it by the end of this month, you would seriously consider moving any planned purchases into the current month. Incentives matter. This was a small-bore bullet; not a boom killer, but a boom wounder. It was missed entirely by the mainstream media. In fact, until I reminded the chairman of the president's Council of Economic Advisors about it on a conference call the following January, he had forgotten about the expiration entirely.

Second is President Bush's decision to shove his vice president aside and triangulate with the Left on environmental policy. While Cheney had been giving some of the most clear-headed and courageous speeches on energy policy in my lifetime, Bush went green. He stopped (and did not pick up again until the very end of his tenure) the push for offshore drilling. He dramatically ramped up alternative energy subsidies, and he raised the regulatory burden on U.S. auto manufacturers by compelling them to raise the fuel efficiency of their most profitable product line, SUVs.

Energy prices rose. Auto profits fell. While the economy showed itself far more resilient than it had in the past at $70 or $80 oil, eventually it broke as oil soared past $100 a barrel and up to $140. Gas at $4 per gallon resulted, and we all know what happened. The second bullet was much larger bore; big enough to bring down a boom, but not quite big enough to bring on a recession.

The third bullet was the Bush administration's toxic mix of mark-to-market accounting mandates and Sarbanes-Oxley's tendency to treat accounting errors as crimes. This was the big one. This is the $5 trillion mistake. This killed the economy.

I did not leave my friends in the investment community, or my friends in the White House, unwarned about this danger. In August 2007, around the time of the first credit crisis, I wrote a memo for a friend in the White House in which I argued that the credit disruptions were not just going to "blow over" and that urgent presidential action was needed. I argued that this action, if taken quickly, could avert a crisis. I argued that a bailout was the wrong approach, that the government did not need to "do something" but to "undo something." I argued for regulatory forbearance. The memo circulated, but did not win the day. I published it in two different articles for *Townhall*. First, I called for the president to take a strong leadership role.

Fox News invited me on to Neil Cavuto's show to make my case, and invited White House spokesman Tony Fratto to respond. Tony, an old friend from the Tom Ridge administration, was as gentlemanly as ever, but in the end his answer was that the White House thought that this would all blow over.

It did not.

Within a year the White House would move from gross underreaction to gross overreaction, from "this will all blow over" to "my hair is on fire, someone blow it out." And still, the fundamental problem remained unaddressed. The Bush administration committed a colossal error in the way it thought about domestic policy; it viewed itself through the prism of the Washington press corps, and believed the story that it was a regime of deregulation and cowboy capitalism. Nothing could have been further from the truth. They failed to adequately heed the warnings of the market, and to identify the free-market solutions to the crisis. This is one of the principal historical causes for the loss of the White House by the GOP and the rise of Barack Obama.

The Republicans, the antigovernment party, went native. It became a party of the government, not the people. Failure came, and paved the way for the biggest government party we've ever seen, the Obama Democrats.

## Our Great Civic Revival

Reform movements can come from above or from below: from the elite level of society or from the grassroots. Typically they come from that segment that, in its particular era, is least corrupt. The various elitist ideologies assume that the repositories of wisdom sit at the top of society, and that renewal must flow down from there. Elitists disagree only on the matter of which top strata—academic, political, creative, executive, priestly, or wealthy—must reform us.

On the other hand, populist ideologies assume that "the people" are incorruptible, and that they alone can purge society of the corruption that always originates at the top.

Providence has not been kind to either view: history has almost as many murderous mobs and bloody uprisings as it does oppressive kings and persecuting popes. Yes, George Washington led a revolt against an oppressive king, but he later defeated the violent Whiskey Rebellion in western Pennsylvania. The same Martin Luther who stood against a corrupt papacy helped the king to stop "the hordes of murderous peasants." The Holocaust came from the top; the Rwandan genocide came from the bottom.

It appears to me that at this moment in American history the populists are more right than the elitists. The people are more wise and virtuous than their leaders.

America, which was designed to be a decentralized republic, has gradually been moving toward centralization during
most of its history, and that trend has accelerated over time. It
is inevitable that a country that moves along a vector of moving
power from the periphery to the center must eventually move
too far.

We seem to have reached such a point. Falling levels of
public confidence in our leadership classes, profound alienation
between the worldviews that obtain between the two, rising
levels of debt and spending, falling levels of economic dyna-
mism, teetering market indicators, increasing enemies abroad,
burgeoning levels of political corruption in high places: all of
these point toward a society that has been poorly governed.

Increasingly large swaths of American society have become
part of a "palace culture" in which wealth and status is tied to
proximity to the center. The great growth industries of our
time are those that receive the favor of the palace: green technology, health and educational bureaucracies, lobbying and
public relations firms, and all of the service businesses that sur-
round the cities that administer these favors, especially Washington, D.C.

Bill Clinton won the 1992 election partly by communicat-
ing this message: "I feel your pain." You, dear reader, can judge
for yourself whether these words were true, whether in fact he
was sufficiently empathetic to feel the pain of events that did
not occur to him. But no one can seriously argue that today's
palace culture does, in fact, actually feel our pain. When we, in
the private sector, lose jobs, they gain jobs. When we face pay
cuts, they get raises. When we are at risk for losing our employment benefits, they receive some of the most lucrative benefits
packages available. As a matter of empirical reality—they do
not feel our pain. The smaller our take-home pay is, the larger

their budgets are. Cranes that used to dot the cityscapes of New York now lift girders in Washington. The incentives are all wrong. Perhaps a Mother Teresa could somehow manage to feel pain for the struggling hinterlands while living among such bounty, but our rulers and their millions of servants are not Mother Teresas.

Palace cultures deform the minds of the members of the party out of power as surely as they do the minds of the party in power. The "loyal opposition" becomes accustomed to living on the crumbs that fall from the table of the king. They find themselves unconsciously bowing and scraping for such scraps, bargaining for more of them. They develop powerful emotional flinches against telling truths about naked emperors.

At such times as this, renewal does not come from minority party elites any more than it comes from majority party ones. It comes from below, from the people themselves. The opposition party leaders will need to learn to follow its followers.

Here's what the followers are saying:

We genuinely expect you to hold to the foundational documents of the Republic. The Declaration of Independence is there to guide us, not just to inspire. Our leaders should read it regularly and know it well. They should imbibe and thoroughly internalize its principles. They should measure all of their actions by it, and reject any that violate its premises. They should not see it as a document to minimize in their reasoning or to work around, but should instead expand its dicta into their permanent mental furniture.

When we ask our leader whether an action is or is not constitutional, we are not engaging in mere rhetorical flourish, we are genuinely asking. We see the

Constitution, as we see the Declaration, as a hedge against tyranny, and a guard of our liberties. We actually require of our leaders that they read the document, to which they each have sworn a sacred oath, often and deeply. We are not satisfied with questions of constitutional legitimacy being fobbed off onto staff. Or kicked down the road for the Supreme Court to deal with at some unspecified date in the future.

They should embrace the limits on government power with the same gusto with which they embrace the grants of power the Constitution enumerates for them.

They should read the bills, every page of every one for which they vote. If a bill is too massive to be read and understood by a member, then it is too massive to be imposed on us.

In times past, when our rulers followed these principles more closely, America was blessed with prosperity undreamt of in the tired annals of mankind. Our knowledge, wealth, science, and health leapfrogged that of civilizations thousands of years older than ours. We caused tyrants to turn worried glances across the great oceans, and eventually to tremble.

We can do all of those things again. We can leap back upon that prosperity curve. We can not only defeat our enemies and our domestic problems, we can, as Ronald Reagan predicted, transcend them.

# Acknowledgments

Humanly speaking, the sine qua non of this project is my good friend Larry Kudlow. My appearances on *The Kudlow Report* led to my initial contact with my literary agent, Giles Anderson, who led me to my editor, Adam Bellow. Both Giles and Adam have been a joy to work with. Giles gently introduced me to the book business, about which I knew virtually nothing. Adam likes to think hard about social and political questions, and our thought sessions were essential to this book.

Over a span of five years, hosting a daily radio program for Tony Renda on Renda Broadcasting created the greatest learning environment I could have imagined. Tony let me actually interview the smartest people in the English-speaking world every day, featuring several hundred economists, historians, biographers, financial analysts, entrepreneurs, and even the occasional philosopher. I couldn't possibly name them all, but those who stand out in my mind, among many others, include such luminaries as Steve Forbes, Alan Meltzer, Brian Wesbury, Bill Bennett, Harvey Mansfield, Rich Karlgaard, Amity Shlaes, Martin Wolf, Brian Lamb, Steve Moore, Alex Chafuen, Seth Lipsky, Marvin Olasky, James Glassman, Ron Morris, and Glen Meakem. All were patient teachers and some have become friends.

Many acts of kindness lie behind this book. I think of Neal Cavuto and his producer Gary Schreier at Fox, and of Glenn Beck, who encouraged me when I appeared on his show back when it was on CNN. Radio hosts such as Rusty Humphries, Ron Morris, Larry Kudlow, and Crane Durham are part of my weekly life. Others, such as Frank Pastore, John Hall, Kathy Emmons, and Don Kroah in the Salem family, have become extended family. Jerry Doyle, Gordon Liddy, Jack Riccardi, and others keep me up to date on current events and how to address them in clear and understandable terms.

Various newspaper and magazine editors have shown various levels of patience with me. Brendan Miniter, Elizabeth Eaves, Nick Schulz, Terry Jeffrey, Jonathan Garthwaite and Chris McEvoy come to mind most easily.

My good friend Vince Birley at Ronald Blue and Company reached out to me and invited me into the Ronald Blue family, where I met Russ Crosson, Scott Houser, and Deborah Kimery and her team. Applying these principles in the real world of investment markets to the advantage of our clients is probably the most satisfying work that I've done in my life.

I thank God for giving me the role of being father to Christopher, Jeremy, Grace, Hope, Mercy, Charlie, and Jack, and father-in-law to Courtney, and most of all for the uncountable joys of being a husband to Susan.

# Index

accounting
    cash-flow, 96
    fair value, 167
    mark-to-market, 47, 200
Acres of Diamonds strategy, 115–18,
    121–22
advertising, transition in, 121
advocacy groups, 170
affinity networks, 56–59, 119–20
agriculture, 152–53
AIG, 6, 177
airline deregulation, 82–83
airlines, subsidies to, 178
Air Southwest, 81
Alinsky, Saul, 41, 128
Allen, Paul, 81
Alternative Minimum Tax (AMT),
    71, 137
amortization, 88
angel investing, 97–109
    as alternate financing arrange-
        ment, 98–99
    and credit crisis, 108
    and legal structure, 107–8
    origin of term, 98
    pooled funding in, 99, 106–7
    by qualified investors, 107–8
Apple Computer, 82
Articles of Confederation, U.S., xii
assets
    dollar-yielding, xviii
    donations of, 74
    shielding, 70
    shifting, xvii
attorney general, U.S., powers of, xiii
autarchies, centrally planned, 40

auto industry, 13–14, 23
    bailouts of, 14, 179
    and fuel efficiency, 200
    government manipulation of,
        34–35

Bacon, Francis, 61
bailouts, 12–15, 177–78, 191
    auto industry, 14, 179
    banking, 167, 177, 186
    and bonds, 178–81
    and interest groups, 177
    social engineering aspect of,
        14–15
banking
    bailout for, 167, 177, 186
    central bank, 44
    deregulation of, 10
    disintegration of financial order,
        55–56, 108
    fractional reserve, 54
    implosion of, 121
    lending in, 123, 185
    minority lending, 47–48
    mortgage markets, 54–55
    nationalization of, 34, 35, 186
    and real estate, 183
    regulation of, 47–48, 120
Bank of America, 39
bankruptcies, 126, 178–81
barter, 50–52
Basic Economics (Sowell), 193
Bass, Harvey, 161–62
Bastiat, Frederick (The Law), 193
Bennett, Bill, 83
Bentsen, Lloyd, 29, 30

Bernanke, Ben S., xiv, 45
Bernstein, Jared, 12, 88
Biden, Joe, 88
blogs
    as high-risk investment, 100
    political, 173
Bodman, Sam, 198
Bolton, Josh, 198
bond counsel, 131, 132
bondholders, 45
bonds
    and bailouts, 178–81
    and bankruptcies, 180
    creditor owners of, 181
    general obligation, 136, 137–38
    and inflation, 127, 140
    moral obligation in, 123–25, 138
    municipal, xvii, 71, 128–38
    muni vs. taxable, 133–35
    revenue, 136–37
    risks of, 123–28
    sewer, 173–74
    spreads in, 141
    and stagflation, 125
    and taxes, 133–37
    time span of, 136
    TIPS, 45–46, 127, 140
bootstrappers, 48–50, 86
Bowyer, Jeremy (son), 193–95
Bowyer, Jerry
    childhood influences on, xiv–xv
    investment principles for the cur-
        rent economy, xvi–xviii
    as optimist, xiv
Braddock, Gentleman Jimmy, 110–11
Brazil, economy of, 47
Brin, Sergey, 48
Brock, David, 155–56
Brooks, David, 169
Buffett, Warren, 147
Built to Last (Roberts), 90
bull market
    political, 168–70, 175
    use of term, 166–67
Bush, George W.
    and bailouts, 13
    and compassionate conservatism, 167
    and credit crisis, 201
    and domestic policy, 201
    and the economy, 195–202
    and media, 195, 201

message discipline of, 6
and minority lending, 48
and oil drilling, 144, 145, 200
and Sarbanes-Oxley, 167, 200–201
tax cuts of, 4, 16, 195–96, 199–200
tax hikes of, 2
Bush Boom, The (Bowyer), 196–98
business
    "Built to Flip," 90–92, 96–97
    global, 119
    initial public offerings, 89, 94, 95
    mergers and acquisitions, 89–97
    relational, 119
    startups, 81–82
    tax "loopholes" of, 88–89
    taxpayer subsidies to, 21
BuzzCharts, 195

calculation, cost of, 167
campaign finance, 28–29, 160–61, 167
cap and trade, 17
capital, mobility of, 111
capital cities, investment in, 176, 191
capital gains, 45, 71, 72, 85–86, 89,
    90, 97, 110
capitalism, free market, 167
capital market disruption, 118
carbon dioxide, 17
Carlson, John, 163
Carter, Jimmy, 30, 43, 81, 82, 125, 144
cash, hoarding, 96
Cash, Johnny, 83
Cavuto, Neil, 201
Central America, leftism in, 38
central planning, 22–24, 40, 43–45
    shift to, 167, 203
Chamberlain, Neville, 26
Chao, Elaine L., 198
Chávez Frías, Hugo, 38, 40–41
Cheney, Dick, 198, 200
Cheney, Lynne, 198
chief of staff, 3
China, and Olympic Games, 113–14
Christian identity politics, 57
Chrysler Corporation, 179–80
Circuit City, 191
civilization, extended order of,
    52–53, 55
Clinton, Bill
    and banking deregulation, 10
    centrism of, 2–3, 8

differences between Obama and,
  2–3, 28, 29–30
and elections, 8
feeling one's pain, 203
and health care, 29–30
and markets, 167
and taxes, 109, 110, 135
Clinton, Hillary, 76–77
CNBC, 39
co-counsel, 131
Colbert, Stephen, 38
cold war, threat of, 27
commodities prices, 148
common law, rules of contract in, 55
commonplaces, 194–95
community affairs consulting, 159–60
Community Reinvestment Act
  (CRA), 47, 167
Compaq, 84
computers
  and productivity, 84–85
  and unemployment, 83–84
Congress, U.S.
  and bailouts, 13–14
  and banking industry, 34
  and elections, 4, 15, 147
  enabling legislation of, 16
  leftward shift of, 167
  and money supply, 185
  and tax hikes, 16
Constitution, U.S.
  on contract law, 55, 125
  as hedge against tyranny, 204–5
  on legislative powers, xiii
  on presidential powers, xii, 16
consumer, as origin of wealth, 20
Consumer Price Index, 127
consumer spending, 140
contract law, 51
  and common law, 55
  Constitution on, 55, 125
  and extended order of civilization,
    52–53
contracts
  broken, 124
  ironclad, 173
  sanctity of, xvii, 54–56, 178, 179
  and tribal bonds, 119
  and trust, 118–19
Conwell, Russell, 115–17, 121–22
corporate communications, 175

corporations
  C-companies, 87
  LLCs, 87
  Subchapter S, 87
  taxes of, 64, 88, 89, 110
cost of goods sold, 118
co-underwriter, 131, 132
court system, U.S., and executive
  powers, xiii
credit card bill, 35
credit crisis, 95, 108, 201
credit unions, 47
currencies, and international investing, 46–47

Daschle, Tom, 31–32
data, meanings of term, 195
debt investment, bonds, 123–28
Declaration of Independence, 204–5
default, risk of, 138, 139–41
deflation, 126–27, 185, 191
democracy, myths of, 113
depreciation, 71, 88–89
documentaries, 164–66
dollars
  inflationary, xvii
  and international investment,
    46–47
Dow Jones Industrial Average
  (DJIA), 187
Dyer, Don, 162

earnings, overtime, 65
economic disintegration, 55–56
economics
  barter, 50–52
  classical, 61
  commodities prices, 148
  free market, 9–10, 141, 143
  supply-side, 196
  trickle-down, 15, 21–23
  trickle-up, 7–8, 12, 22
*Economics in One Lesson* (Hazlitt), 193
economies of scale, 78, 94
economy
  and Bush, 195–202
  centrally planned vs. free, xvi, 1, 22
  and Fabianism, 1
  growth of, 15, 27, 43, 140, 198
  minimum wage, 143
  monetary vs. tax policy, 43–44

economy *(cont.)*
　and public spending, 4
　redistribution philosophy, 7–9,
　　10, 21
　stimulus to, 4, 12, 15, 186, 191
　supply disruptions, 144–52
　and taxes, 27
　and unemployment, 79–80, 143
　wage and price controls, 35,
　　143–44
education
　alternative systems of, 104–5
　"A Nation at Risk," 83
　inferior products of, 85
　money made in, 129
　vocational vs. liberal arts, 104
election process, 171–73
Ellison, Larry, 48, 82
Emanuel, Rahm, 3
Endangered Species Act, 17
energy costs, 82
energy grids, 149, 151
energy sector, nationalization of, 34,
　35
energy supply disruption, 118,
　144–52
engineers, 131–32
England, Gordon, 198
Enron, 95
entitlements, middle-class, 139
entrepreneurs
　advertising by, 121
　and angel investors, 106–7
　bootstrappers, 48–50, 86
　and employment, 80
　financial controls of, 65
　sole proprietorships, 87
　strategic, 92
　and taxes, 75–79, 85–86, 89
　and wealth creation, 97
EPA (Environmental Protection
　Agency), 17
equity, 124
ETFs (exchange-traded funds), 72,
　136, 189
extended order of civilization,
　52–53, 55

Fabian socialism, xv, 1
Fannie Mae, 129
FCC, 156, 157

Federal Open Market Committee
　(FOMC), xiii, 45
Federal Reserve System, powers of,
　xiii–xiv, 44, 184–85
FedEx, 81, 82, 83, 89, 152
Fed funds rate, 184
Fisher, Jon, 92
food industry, prices in, 35–36
Ford, Gerald R., 43, 125
foreclosure, 55
foreign markets, xvii
Fox News, 156, 163, 201
Fratto, Tony, 201
Freddie Mac, 129
Friedman, Milton, 44

Gates, Bill, 81, 86
Geithner, Tim, 3–4
General Electric (GE), 39
General Motors (GM), 34, 39, 177
geography, 150, 151–52, 190
Gilder, George, 84
global competition, 110–14, 140,
　167–68
Global Crossing, 95
global finance, 120
global sourcing, 150
Golconda, diamond mine of, 116
Google, 48
government
　bailouts from, 13–14, 167,
　　177–78
　bankruptcy of, 137
　careers in, 168, 171–73, 191
　as consuming entity, 16
　debt of, 139
　entitlements to services from, xii
　expansionist, 39
　market interventions by, xvi, 4,
　　36–37
　minimal, xii
　poor, 203
　pressures from, 39–40
　propaganda from, 39
　public spending, 4
　purchasing power of, xii–xiii
　regulatory regime of, 34, 47, 62, 82,
　　94, 95, 120, 153, 161–62, 167–68
　resistance to encroachment by,
　　40–41
　right to petition, 162

roles of, xii
subsidies from, 101, 129, 177–78, 189
gradualism, strategy of, 1, 12
Great Depression, xiv, xv, 5
green agenda, 190
Gregoire, Christine, 162

Hafed, Ali, 116
Harwood, John, 145–46
Hayek, Friedrich, 61
  *The Fatal Conceit,* 52, 55
  *The Road to Serfdom,* 36–37
Hazlitt, Henry, 193
health care
  and Clintons, 29–30, 76–77
  corporate costs of, 32, 33
  financing system for, 33–34
  nationalization of, 28–35
  Obamacare, xi, 16–17, 64, 77
  reversal of, 15, 32
  small business costs of, 33, 77
  and taxes, 63, 77
  universal, 139
health savings accounts (HSAs), 63
*Heaven on Earth* (Muravchik), 37
hedge funds, 147
hoarding, 43–44
Holocaust, 202
Home Depot, 187
housing market, 183
Huckabee, Mike, 57
human rights, suppression of, 40

identity politics, 56
*In an Uncertain World* (Rubin), 29, 30
incentives, 200, 204
India, investment in, 111, 114
inflation, xvii, 190
  and bonds, 127, 140
  and COLAs, 191
  default via, 139
  and loose money, 43
  as monetary phenomenon, 44, 186
  and risk, 138–41
  stagflation, 44–45
  TIPS, 45–46, 127, 140
  and wage and price controls, 35
inflation tax, 44
initial public offerings (IPOs), 89, 94, 95

Interior Department, U.S., 144
Internet
  as cost-cutting tool, 100–101
  investment in, 173, 174
  media model destroyed by, 121
  and regulation, 153
investment
  angel, 97–109
  bathwater, 99–101
  bonds, 123–28
  due diligence in, 66, 106, 177, 181
  in emerging markets, 46
  international, 46–47, 111, 114, 141
  local, 116–22
  in media, 173–75, 176
  no-friends-and-family policy, 99
  as political backer, 172–73
  in politically favored technology, 14–15
  in real estate, 181–92
  retail, 12
  and retirement planning, 68–70
  risk sharing in, 106–7
  sewer bonds, 173–74
  in socialism, 67–68
  supersafe portfolio, 127
  and taxes, 62–73
investment principles, xvi–xviii
Iraq, 113
IRAs, 69
*It's a Wonderful Life* (movie), 54

Jackson, Alphonso, 198
Japan
  ghost economy of, 25–27
  recession in, 125–27
J-curve, 111–14, *115*
Jefferson, Thomas, 61
Jewish Diaspora, 120
Jobs, Steve, 82, 86
job security, 79
Johnson, Lyndon B., 30, 81
Johnson, Paul, 27

Karlgaard, Rich, 48–49, 81–82
Kelleher, Herb, 81
Keynesian central planning model, 22, 43, 44, 140
King, Rollin, 81

Krugman, Paul, 198
Kudlow, Larry, 195
labor unions
    and automation, 83
    and bailouts, 177, 178, 179
    and energy policy, 147–48
    government support of, 16
    and home-based business, 77
    and Obama's election, 80
    and public sector, 129, 132
    recruitment by, 80
    and unemployment, 79
    violence of, 38
Laffer, Arthur, 61, 64
Laffer Curve, 112–13
land-use laws, 149
Law, The (Bastiat), 193
Lay, Ken, 95
Lazear, Ed, 199
leftism, xvi, 2
"Legend of John Henry, The," 83
legislative bypass operations, xiii
Lehman, John, 198
Lenin, V. I., 76, 146
Levitt, Arthur, 95
Lewis, Ken, 39
liberation theolory, 41
liberties, positive vs. negative, xii
Liles, Bill, 161–62
lizard brain, use of term, 182
lobbying business, 170
Locke, John, 61
Lowe's, 187
loyal opposition, 204
Luther, Martin, 59, 202

macroeconomics, 85
Madison, James, 61
Madoff, Bernie, 56–59, 95
Manifesto for Media Freedom,
        A (Anderson and Thierer),
        155–56, 161–63
Marconi, Guglielmo, 153
mark-to-market accounting, 47, 200
Matthews, Chris, 101
McCain, John, 57
McCain-Feingold bill, 167, 171
McCaskill, Claire, 88
McEvoy, Chris, 195
media
    advertising in, 121

alternative, 100–101
and audience preferences, 164
in capital cities, 176, 191
and community affairs consulting,
    159–60
documentaries, 164–66
DVD distribution, 166
and "fairness" lobby, 155–57
FM radio, 163–64
and freedom of expression, 158,
    162–63
heritage broadcast stations, 153
influence of, 201
intimidation against, 29, 38, 39
investment in, 173–75, 176
professional insulters in, 38
propaganda in, 38–39
regulation of, 153, 154, 156–59
resistance to autocracy in, 41
revenue streams of, 154
suppression of, 153–66
talk radio, 160–65
traditional model of, 121
Media Matters for America, 155–56
Medicaid, 167
Medicare, 89
mergers and acquisitions (M&A),
        89–97
Microsoft, 81–82
militarism, 40
Miner, Bob, 82
Mineta, Norm Y., 198
minimum wage, 143
Mises, Ludwig von, 55–56, 61
monetary policy vs. tax policy, 43–45
money creation, 46–47, 86
money supply, control of, xiii–xiv,
        139, 184–86
monopolies, 82, 83, 153
mortgage finance system, 129
mortgage markets, 54–55
mortgages, subprime, 183–84
municipal bonds, xvii, 71, 128–38
Muravchik, Joshua, 37
mutual funds, 72, 136, 187, 189

nationalization, xvii, 13, 37, 62
national unity, 9
"Nation at Risk, A" (Bennett), 83
negative liberties, xii
New Deal, 128

New Era, 124
New Era Foundation, 57–58
Nixon, Richard M., 43, 81, 125
nonprofit sector, 73–75
nursing home industry, 80

Oates, Ed, 82
Obama, Barack
    autobiography of, 19–20
    on business subsidies, 13–14
    calm demeanor of, 5
    and central planning, 44–45
    differences between Clinton and,
        2–3, 28, 29–30
    and the economy, xvi, 6–9, 10–11,
        19–23, 137
    and elections, 8
    energy policy of, 144–47
    as Fabian socialist, 1
    and labor unions, 80
    and media regulation, 156–59
    moral universe of, 20
    and nonprofit sector, 73–74
    and presidential powers, xii–xiii, 16
    press conferences of, 8, 10–11, 13
    proximity to, 30–32
    and public works, 128–29, 135, 171
    reasoning processes of, 5–6, 7–9,
        11–12
    rise of, 202
    and small business, 77, 86–89
    and tax cuts, 7, 11, 64–65
    and tax hikes, 1–2, 10, 16, 63–64,
        88, 90, 109–10, 135–36
    and utopians, 170
Obama, Michelle, 73–74
Obamacare, xi, 16–17, 64, 77
Office of Management and Budget
    (OMB), 4
offshore drilling, 190
oil prices, 200
opposition party, 204
Oracle, 48, 82
Orszag, Peter, 4
outsourcing shops, 80

Page, Larry, 48
Paul, Saint, 20
Paulson, Henry, 3
Pets.com, 91
*Philadelphia Inquirer*, 100

philanthropy, 74
Phillips, A. W., 22
Phillips Curve, 22
Plato, and the soul, 182
Podesta, John, 156
polar bears, 17
political consulting, 172–73
political economy, science of, 143
political fund-raising, 175
political theory, 61
politicization, 171
politics
    backers in, 172–73
    business of, 170–71, 173
    central authority, 177
    local, 172
Ponzi schemes, 56–59
populism, 21, 76, 108–9, 120, 202
positive liberties, xii
post office, 83
Potter, Harry, 25–27
power, policy as about, 128
president
    powers of, xii–xiii, 16
    proximity to, 30
    and staff positions, 3
price floors, 143–44
private activity bonds, 71
productivity, 44
    and economies of scale, 78
    and information technology, 84–85
    and labor costs, 85
professionals, financial controls of, 65
professional services, shopping for, 105
propaganda, 37–40
protectionism, 119
public careers, talent shift to, 168
public debt, 132–33, 171
public policy
    careers in, 168, 171–73
    influencing, 170–71
public-private partnerships, 178
public relations, 175
public transit, 178
Putin, Vladimir, 114

Reagan, Ronald, 5, 17, 109, 110, 205
real estate, 175–77, 181–92
real estate partnerships, 192
redistribution, 7–9, 10, 21
reform, alternatives to, xvi–xvii

reform movements, 202
refuge, cities of, xvii
Reich, Robert, 39
REITs, 187–89
Rendell, Ed, 100
retail real estate, 191–92
retirement planning, 68–70
Rice, Condoleezza, 198
risk aversion, 26, 27
risk capital, 48
risk sharing, 106–7
Romer, Christina, 4
Romney, Mitt, 57
Roosevelt, Franklin D., 5, 30
Roth IRAs, 69
Rothschild network, 120
Rove, Karl, 30–31, 199
Rubin, Robert, 29, 30
Rukeyser, Louis, 120
Rumsfeld, Donald H., 198
Russia, Bolsheviks in, 113–14
Rwandan genocide, 202

Salam, Reihan, 169
Sandinistas, 38
Sarbanes-Oxley Act (2002), 94, 110, 167, 197, 200–201
Savings Bonds, Series I, 45
Say, J. B., 61
schedule C income, 72
school vouchers, 129
Service Employees International Union (SEIU), 39, 80
Shaffer, Allen, 6
Shakespeare, William, 61
small business, 13
  family-owned, 75
  and health care, 33, 77
  home-based, 77
  partnership income in, 75
  pension plans in, 69
  as personal wealth-building strategy, 78
  as politically protected class, 70
  Schedule C deductions in, 75, 88
  start-up, 75–79, 86–89, 97, 106
  structure of, 87–88
  taking from, to give to the rich, 14, 15
  and taxes, 74–75, 86–89, 109, 199
Smith, Adam, 61

Smith, Fred, 81, 89
Snow, John, 198
social capital, 19
socialism
  British Labour, 37
  as chaos, 61–62
  in Clinton era, 110
  domestic pressure groups in, 37
  Fabian, xv, 1
  false promises of, xviii
  food shortages in, 36
  gradualist, 12
  *Heaven on Earth* (Muravchik) on, 37
  investment in, 67–68
  nationalization in, 37
  peasant extermination in, 36
  propaganda in, 37–40
  of western Europe, 26
social pressure, 51
Social Security, 64, 89, 110
software, as front-loaded cost business, 49
sole proprietorships, 87
Soros, George, 155–56
Southwest Airlines, 81, 82, 83
Sowell, Thomas, 193
spending patterns, 12
spreads, 141
stability, loss of, 113
stagflation, 44–45, 89, 124–25
Stewart, Jon, 38
stimulus plans, 4, 12, 15, 186, 191
stockholders, 45
  and bailouts, 177, 178
  and bankruptcies, 179, 180, 181
  risks of, 123–24
stocks
  equity investments in, 123, 143–92
  negative returns on, 125
  and stagflation, 125
"Stop the Presses" (Bowyer), 197
*Strategic Entrepreneurism* (Fisher), 92
subsidies
  preliminaries to, 13
  smart-bomb, 177–78
substitution effect, 62, 148
Summers, Lawrence, 4, 8–10
supply management, 150
TARP (Troubled Asset Relief Program), 180

tax code
rebalancing, 11
for social engineering, 67
tax cuts
of Bush, 4, 16, 195–96, 199–200
and Obama, 7, 11, 64–65
public response to, 65
tax efficiency, 71–73
taxes
alternative minimum, 71, 137
and bonds, 133–37
capital gains, 45, 71, 72, 85–86,
89, 90, 97, 110
of corporations, 64, 88, 89, 110
and economic growth, 27
effective tax rate, 64
and entrepreneurship, 75–79,
85–86, 89
focus on, 62–73
and health care, 63, 77
income, 72–73, 90, 110
of individuals, 110
inheritance, 73
and investment, 62–73
and Laffer Curve, 112–13
loopholes, 88–89
payroll, 64, 72, 75, 110
and small business, 74–75, 86–89,
109, 199
and transfer payments, 7, 21,
64–65, 66
tax-free income, 133
tax hikes
and bonds, 135–36
and Bush (2003), 2
and deficit hawks, 4
and Obama, 1–2, 10, 16, 63–64,
88, 90, 109–10, 135–36
tax policy vs. monetary policy, 43–45
tax returns, outside preparer of, 67, 87
tax shelters, 71–72
Tea Parties, xi, 41
temp agencies, 80
Thatcher, Margaret, 37
Thierer, Adam, 155–56, 161–63
think tanks, 170
TIPS (Treasury Inflation-Protected
Securities), 45–46, 127, 140
Tocqueville, Alexis de, 61
Toll Brothers, 187
trade agreements, 120

transfer payments, 23
to consumers, 13
to middle class, 7, 10
from small business, 14
and taxes, 7, 21, 64–65, 66
transportation, 17, 118, 151–52
Treasury Bonds, U.S., 139
Treasury Department, U.S., 3–4
tribalism, 56, 119
Truman, Harry S., 30
trust, 118–20
trust funds, 75
Tyco, 95
Tyson, Mike, 111

UAW (United Auto Workers), 14,
177, 179
unemployment, 79–80
and computers, 83–84
and minimum wage, 143
teenage, 143
unions. *See* labor unions

venture capital, 91, 98, 147

wage and price controls, 35, 36, 143–44
wage inflation, 85
Wagoner, Rick, 34
*Wall Street Week* (TV show), 120
Walmart, 80
war, as solution, 40
Washington, D.C., as company town,
168, 190–91, 203
Washington, George, 202
wealth, creation of, 20, 21, 43, 75, 78, 97
*Wealth and Poverty* (Gilder), 84
wealth preservation, intergenera-
tional, 73, 75
welfare state, 27, 79
Wesbury, Brian, 95, 124, 125
western Europe, 26–27
Whiskey Rebellion, 202
Wilbur, Kirby, 163
WorldCom, 95
World War I, 27
World War II, 27, 37
Wozniak, Steve, 82
Wriston, Walter, 111

Zinsmeister, Karl, 199
Zipf, Robert, 134

# About the Author

Jerry Bowyer is Senior Economist for Ronald Blue and Company, a financial services firm, and a CNBC contributor, where he appears on *Kudlow and Company* regularly. He is also a frequent guest on radio.

Jerry has also served as the chief economist to Benchmark Financial Network. Prior to his work at Benchmark, he was a financial and tax accountant with a Big Six accounting firm, founded one of the most successful economic think tanks in America, the Allegheny Institute for Public Policy, and served as the chairman of the board of Impact Total Return Portfolio, a four-star-rated mutual fund, where he was also chairman of its investment committee.

Jerry has been a guest professor and/or guest lecturer at Carnegie Mellon University, the University of Pittsburgh, and Saint Vincent College, as well as a commencement speaker at his alma mater, Robert Morris. He is the founder of Bowyer Media, which produces radio and television programs, and has been quoted by and/or written for the *New York Times*, the *New York Sun*, the *Wall Street Journal*, *Newsweek*, the *Washington Post*, and the *International Herald Tribune*. He also writes regularly for Forbes.com, National Review Online, Human Events, Townhall.com, TechCentralStation.com, and *Townhall* magazine.